The Significant Life

Overcoming Your Fear
of Being Unnoticed and Forgotten

George M. Weaver

To Tehwan &
Tom

George Weaver
Matt. 10:30-31

CROSSLINK
PUBLISHING

The Significant Life

ⅅ CrossLink Publishing
ℂ www.crosslinkpublishing.org

ISBN 978-1-936746-61-3

Library of Congress Control Number: 2013940933

Table of Contents

Dedicated to my family
LeAnne, Mary & Michael Weaver—
You inspire me every day

Preface

This book addresses the need and struggle of individual people to be noticed and remembered by others. In addition to many celebrities and prominent persons, we'll meet the little-known John Ledyard, who in the 1700s sought to attain fame by becoming the first person to walk around the world. His efforts cost him his life at the age of thirty-seven. Before dying, he said, "A blush of generous regret sits on my Cheek to hear of any Discovery there that I have not [had] part in."[1]

We'll also meet Arthur Bremer, a twenty-one-year-old unemployed busboy who was alienated from his family and had no friends. He kept a diary of his efforts to gain fame by assassinating a well-known public official. He first targeted President Richard Nixon and then Alabama Governor George Wallace. Bremer claimed in his diary: "I'm as important as the Start of WWI just need the little opening & a second of time."[2]

How can we explain this yearning to be noticed and remembered? And is there any way to satisfy it?

The universe is brimming with activity, and each of us forms a very small part of it. Think back one hundred years, one thousand years, five thousand years. Other events were occurring then, and none of us was a part of them. They are now gone and mostly forgotten.

Soon the activities of today will also be gone and forgotten. There will be other events in the future of which none of us will be a part. And they too will quickly end and be forgotten. In one hundred years, how many times a day will my name be mentioned among other people even on this small planet we call home? Will any people think of me at all? How about in one thousand years? Probably not.

And what would it mean for someone to think of me in one hundred years or one thousand years? Suppose that in the distant future, while browsing a dusty genealogy or computer file, an archives clerk stumbles across my name, that is the collection of English language characters by which I'm referred to today. Would that clerk be thinking of me? Not really.

Uncomfortable at the prospect of oblivion, each of us, consciously or unconsciously, is on a desperate quest to leave a mark or legacy on this world. There are those who seem to have made a mark so far beyond my level as to be otherworldly. Examples are Henry Ford and Walt Disney, whose names appear to be permanently and everywhere preserved through the businesses they founded, the Ford Motor Company and the Walt Disney Company. Other persons from this realm are George Washington and Abraham Lincoln. Their names and faces—on a worldwide scale—adorn money, postage stamps, buildings, universities, cities, and even places they never visited. And there are persons who are recognized by a single word or name—Aristotle, Augustus, Elvis, Madonna, and Bono. Still others are known merely by their initials—JFK, MLK, and LBJ.

I could never aspire to that kind of mark or legacy. But my neighbor gets his name in the paper, my cousin earns a spot on the swim team, an old friend makes a list of successful entrepreneurs or gets a prestigious job. What about me? Do I have any importance? Will I get any recognition? Will I be remembered when I'm gone? I hate to think of being gone. Surely, I can't die before I have left my mark.

There are many human needs. Food, water, clothing, and shelter are the most obvious. We also need love, human affection, and sexual satisfaction. Beyond these immediate needs are ultimate needs of purpose (or meaning) and significance.

The goal of this writing is to consider the significance of each of us as an individual person. The significance of the individual as opposed to that of humanity forms our topic because the basic human reality is the individual, not humanity or humankind. In fact, the category of humanity approaches an abstraction in that each human being is physically distinct from all of the rest of humanity.

By "significance," I mean the extent to which each of us is known, appreciated, influential, and will be remembered. The word "importance" will be used interchangeably with significance.

Although some people use the word "significance" as equivalent to "purpose" or "meaning," I wish to separate the question of the purpose or meaning of a human life from that of its individual significance. Generally, "purpose" means having a reason for being or directed at a goal. In our thinking, we often extend this to the idea of having a useful or worthy reason for being or directed at a useful or worthy goal. But this is not the same as being known, appreciated, influential, and remembered.

This desire to be known, appreciated, influential, and remembered seems to operate independently of the desire for purpose or meaning. If the purpose of a human life were x or y or nothing at all, people would still desire to be known, appreciated, influential, and remembered.

A life that is purposeful could be insignificant, and a life that is significant could be purposeless. For instance, a single individual earthworm lives a purposeful but insignificant life as it silently churns the soil. There are apparently no conscious observers to whom the solitary earthworm is known, who appreciate it, are influenced by it, and will remember it. By contrast, Hitler's life was significant, in that it was known by many observers, appreciated by some, influential over millions, and remembered by many—but horribly misguided and ultimately purposeless (i.e., it did not serve a worthy purpose).

The difference in these concepts is evident, moreover, from considering that, according to Christianity, all humans have the same purpose—"to glorify God and to enjoy Him forever."[3] But that same purpose applies to all seven billion of us now walking the planet and the even greater billions who have gone before. We all have this same purpose even if one accepts the notion that God has a different blueprint or plan for how each person should fit into an overall mosaic of glorifying Him. So, if one person disappears, the overarching purpose of glorifying God is still well-served. But what is my individual significance as against this mass of humanity? Would anything be lost if I disappeared or had never been born?

The difference in purpose and significance, as I am using these terms, is also apparent from another angle. Under the teachings of Christianity, it will be seen that every human being stands fully significant (in the sense of being known, appreciated, influential, and remembered) whether or not he is a Christian. A person may reject Christ and thus not serve the purpose of glorifying God. But, as we will see, if Christianity is true, a person cannot cease being significant.

The Christian answer to the problem of the purpose or meaning of human life has been widely discussed in many works, among them the wildly popular *The Purpose Driven Life* by Rick Warren and the more recent *The Call* by Os Guinness. But the subject of this inquiry, the individual significance of each of us, has received much less discussion.

I hope to show that, for those of us who have not fully appreciated them before, Christian doctrines establishing the significance of each individual person are like an uncashed check or unscratched winning lottery ticket for one million dollars. It's yours, it's in your wallet, but you've never spent it or even recognized it.

I started this lifelong journey of understanding by seeing the lives of family members cut short. I watched my father become disabled after working only a few brief years and then die several years later at the age of forty-five from a brain tumor. He never had time to establish a career and died while his children were still young. I also agonized over the three-year battle and then death of my first wife, Allison, at age thirty-seven from breast cancer. She did not have a career and never bore children. When the disease was closing in, Allison shared with me one of her deepest fears: "If I die, I'll be forgotten." By human standards, neither was significant or important, and each was long ago left behind in the ever-flowing river of events. I hope to show in this book, however, that they and the countless others with similar stories are fully significant—no less than if they had lived long and famous lives.

Section I:

The Apparent Insignificance
of the Individual Person

1. Unhappily Insignificant

There is no remembrance of earlier things;
And also of the later things which will occur,
There will be for them no remembrance
Among those who will come later still.
                                        —Ecclesiastes 1:11

Time like an ever rolling stream bears all her sons away.
They fly forgotten as a dream dies at the break of day.
    —Isaac Watts, "O God Our Help in Ages Past" (1719)

Against the infinities of space and time each of us is apparently utterly insignificant. In terms of space, the individual human disappears in the incomprehensible size of the universe. The body of a person fills only a few cubic feet of space, and his senses are able to survey only a slightly larger area. One can get lost even in his own house—in the range of his senses. And he forms but a pencil point in a world that measures twenty-five thousand miles in circumference and teems with the incessant activity of more than seven billion people. Further, the earth itself is almost imperceptible in this vast universe, which stretches billions of light years. As Nikos Kazantzakis says in *Zorba the Greek*, we are all "minute grubs on the small leaf of a tremendous tree," and only a few of us ever even "reach the edge of the leaf."[1]

Certainly there are advantages to our spatial limitations. If you get bored with me, for example, you can leave the room and get away

3

from me. But the negative aspect is that each of us is shudderingly insignificant.

Time is the other infinity in which the individual person is lost. Have you ever mistakenly typed into a document the designation for the current year—instead of 2013, perhaps the year 300, 5003, or 20013—and then wondered what life or the earth was or will be like at that distant time? This underscores the narrow window of time that each of us occupies.

The big things we enjoy, and the little things too, are fleeting or ephemeral. The hot shower, sexual intimacy, a good meal, a glass of wine, dessert, vacation, Christmas day. An event disappears so quickly that the anticipation seems more enduring, that is, longer and persistent, than the event itself. On the third day of a vacation, for example, a cloud slowly descends. We know the vacation will soon be over. After the halfway point, gloom hits. What we had once looked forward to with great anticipation will soon join our faded memories, as the wrinkle in the space-time continuum we call the present inexorably moves forward. Even events of longer duration—such as a career, marriage, or child rearing— become a blur when they are past. Popular singer-songwriter Kenny Loggins describes the passage of time in "Watching the River Run":

> And it goes on and on, watching the river run,
> Further and further from things that we've done,
> Leaving them one by one.
> And we have just begun watching the river run.

The average life span, seventy to eighty years, is a bare, unrepeated, faint flicker in the never-ending flow of time. We are like seeds in the wind. One person's life is nothing even in the few thousand years of recorded human history. The Bible graphically describes the transience of the individual human's lifespan as "grass [or] a flower of the field" that appears and blooms in the morning and is gone by the same afternoon (Psalm 103:15-16; Psalm 90:5-6; 1 Peter 1:24). It also paints transience with the images of a "shadow" (1 Chronicles 29:15), "vapor" (James 4:14), "mere breath" (Psalm 39:5, 11), a weaver's "shuttle" (Job 7:6), and "smoke from a chimney" (Hosea 13:3).

In the Venerable Bede's eighth-century *Ecclesiastical History of the English People*, the author captures the transience of life with a memorable image:

> [W]hen we compare the present life of man on earth with that time of which we have no knowledge, it seems to me like the swift flight of a single sparrow through the banqueting-hall where you are sitting at dinner on a winter's day with your thegns and counsellors. In the midst there is a comforting fire to warm the hall; outside, the storms of winter rain or snow are raging. This sparrow flies swiftly in through one door of the hall, and out through another. While he is inside, he is safe from the winter storms, but after a few moments of comfort, he vanishes from sight into the wintry world from which he came. Even so, man appears on earth for a little while; but of what went before this life or of what follows, we know nothing.[2]

And what hurts most is that after we are gone the sun will still rise and set, people will live and die, laugh and cry just as if we had never been here.

Each of us is aware of the whole expanse of space and time, yet each is an exceedingly small and transient part of it. Animals are not troubled by their similar limitations: "The worm feeds sweetly till he is no longer remembered" (Job 24:20). But no person is satisfied to vanish like a vapor when his days are finished. All of us have a deep fear of oblivion. Illustrating this fear, we are, for instance, disturbed by accounts of the mass anonymous graves of those killed in battle or reports of burials at sea, as when the countless soldiers who died in 1918 from the Great Influenza while crossing the Atlantic were unceremoniously "consigned nameless to the sea."[3]

We all feel that the sum of knowledge, appearance, foibles, personality, ideas, and humor that makes each of us unique must somehow be preserved. Each of us feels deeply that there is a singular importance to his or her existence that must not be lost. Os Guinness says that despite the vicissitudes of life "we intuitively act and think as if we have supreme value."[4] If one loses his newspaper he can buy another, if he wrecks his car or his dog dies he can find a suitable replacement, but when a person dies something irreplaceable is lost. Another person can be found to do his job and assume his societal functions, but that unique intersection of characteristics that forms the individual person has disappeared. Each of us sees himself as slipping away while nobody notices or cares. Indeed, we seem to disappear like canoes that make no sound and leave no wake.

But we fiercely struggle against disregard of our individual uniqueness and singularity. Individual humans are not concerned so much about the survival of the species as they are about their personal survival or significance. In order to push ourselves beyond our confining space-time limits, we as individuals try to set ourselves apart from the rest of humanity. It is unsettling to admit that one is average or ordinary—a routine person. We like to think of the public as everyone but us. We, especially, are not mere faces in the crowd.

Celebrities form a laboratory of people who are desperate to be noticed. Salvador Dali once said, "The thought of not being recognized [is] unbearable."[5] Actor Charlie Sheen spoke for many when he said, "All I wanted was to be liked, recognized, included. I didn't want to be just a face in the crowd."[6] Brigette Bardot expressed her desire for recognition this way: "Time will destroy me one day, as it destroys everything. But no one else will ever be Bardot. I am the only Bardot, and my species is unique."[7] Lady Gaga sings, "I live for the applause, applause, applause . . . the way that you cheer and scream for me." She adds in another song, "yes we live for the Fame, Doin' it for the Fame, Cuz we wanna live the life of the rich and famous."

Even the famously reclusive Greta Garbo made sure she was famous before she decided to shun publicity. This follows the pattern of many literary figures, such as the English poet John Keats, who seem both to seek and to disdain fame. One commentator describes this as striving "for a virtually anonymous fame."[8]

This appetite for attention leads us in many directions. Next we'll explore some of these.

Questions for Reflection

1. Against the vast scope of time and space, does the individual person appear to have any significance—in the sense of being known, appreciated, influential, and remembered? Why or why not?

2. Do you ever feel small and unnoticed? Do you worry that you'll be forgotten after you die? Do you ever feel a need to leave a mark or legacy on the world? Do you believe that leaving a mark or legacy is necessary for you to be a worthwhile person? Explain your answers.

3. Are most persons content to be unnoticed and forgotten? Are animals bothered by this? Why do you think so?

4. What biblical metaphors best describe the brevity of the individual person's life?

5. Reread the quotes from celebrities who seem driven by the desire for fame and attention. How would you respond to them?

2. Efforts at Significance, Part One

The scribes and the Pharisees . . . do all their deeds to be noticed by men.

—Matthew 23:2-5

There was a certain man named Simon, who was . . . claiming to be someone great; and they all . . . were giving attention to him.

—Acts 8:9-10

But who is there to notice us? Modern man, doubting that any god exists, is left with the frightening belief that people are the only observers in the universe. There is seemingly no other consciousness to notice and remember us. As a result, the usual target of our attempts at significance is other finite human minds.

In his exhaustive history of human fame, Leo Braudy documents how the appetite for fame shifted from heavenly to earthly venues when the existence of God and life after death came under widespread doubt after the Middle Ages.[1] But the focus on earthly opportunities for attention is not new. Even when Jesus walked the earth He indicted the scribes and Pharisees for "do[ing] all their deeds to be noticed by men" (Matthew 23:2-5).

Most of us see impressing other people as the only way of living past our finite senses and physical death. Spanish philosopher-poet Miguel de Unamuno describes "this tremendous struggle to singularize ourselves, to survive in some way in the memory of others and of posterity."[2] Napoleon echoed these sentiments: "Guess what they are holding out to me. The salvation of my soul? But as far as I am concerned, there is no immortality but the memory that is left in the minds of men."[3] He also said, "History I conquered rather than studied."[4]

The Roman orator Cicero was also consumed by the desire to be noticed by other people. According to one expert, Cicero had an obsessive "need to accumulate repetitions of his name in public as a psychic bank balance." Looking to the future, he asked of his associate Atticus, " 'What will history say of me a thousand years hence?' "[5]

But the fallibility and mortality of human minds make it desirable to leave a more permanent record. We are surrounded by things more permanent than we—topographical features, buildings, monuments, books, records. So we try to attach ourselves to them. We attempt to turn our intangible actions, speech, and thoughts into tangible, nonperishable things that can be seen by others. Hannah Arendt puts it this way:

> They [speech and thought] themselves do not produce, bring forth anything, they are as futile as life itself. In order to become worldly things, that is deeds and facts and events and patterns of thoughts or ideas, they must first be seen, heard, and remembered and then transformed, reified as it were, into things—into sayings of poetry, the written page or the printed book,

into paintings or sculpture, into all sorts of records, documents, and monuments.[6]

Unamuno says we "[act] in such a way that we make ourselves irreplaceable, in impressing our seal and mark upon others."[7]

There are many ways in which we try to climb outside of our space-time limits and leave a record in the minds of other persons or make a mark on our surroundings. These could be described as ways of seeking fame or a substitute for it. Let's look at some examples of the things we do.

Reaching a Position or Accomplishment That Sets One Apart

One of the primary forms that this quest for significance takes is seeking to attain a position or reach an accomplishment that no or few others have. This is made possible by human recognition of hierarchies and our appetite for superlatives. In the words of William Law, to "be attended with splendor and equipage . . . to have titles of dignity, to be above our fellow creatures, to command the bows and obeisance of other people, to be looked on with admiration" are among "the great, the honorable, the desirable things to which the spirit of the world turns the eyes of all people."[8]

There are hundreds of titles that seem to set the titleholder apart from those who don't have the title—professor, doctor, captain, editor, author, elder, reverend, president, chairman, father, senator, mayor, governor, chief, pilot, director, master, etc.

At the funeral of the dowager Queen Elizabeth (affectionately known as the Queen Mum) in 2002, her British titles, which were only a subset of her total titles, were read aloud.[9] The celebrant intoned:

> Thus it hath pleased Almighty God to take out of this transitory life unto His Divine Mercy the late Most High, Most Mighty and Most Excellent Princess Elizabeth, Queen Dowager and Queen Mother, Lady of the Most Noble Order of the Garter, Lady of the Most Ancient and Most Noble Order of the Thistle, Lady of the Imperial Order of the Crown of India, Grand Master and Dame Grand Cross of the Royal Victorian Order upon whom had been conferred the Royal Victorian Chain, Dame Grand Cross of the Most Excellent Order of the British Empire, Dame Grand Cross of the Most Venerable Order of the Hospital of St John of Jerusalem, Relict of His Majesty King George the Sixth and Mother of Her Most Excellent Majesty Elizabeth The Second by the Grace of God of the United Kingdom of Great Britain and Northern Ireland and of her other Realms and Territories Queen, Head of the Commonwealth, Defender of the Faith, Sovereign of the Most Noble Order of the Garter, whom may God preserve and bless with long life, health and honour and all worldly happiness.[10]

This is one of the most striking collection of titles that can be imagined.

For those of us without an aristocratic pedigree, businesses stand ready to sell titles to anyone. These titles fall into two categories, effective and seated titles. The seated titles cost more and include a token interest in real estate. Along with the promise of expedited social climbing and preferential treatment in public accommodations, these merchants offer "documentation" for the titles Sir, Lord, Lady, Baron, Baronness, Count, Countess, Earl, Viscount, Viscountess, Marquess, Marchionness, and others.[11] One website offers a special time-limited, half-price discount package of "two titles for any two people" upon payment of $294 by credit card (or PayPal).[12]

Yet other people make false claims of royal lineage, often presenting themselves as lost heirs to a throne. After the Roman emperor Nero's suicide in AD 68, there was a "crop of false Neros."[13] Ironically, "it was the twentieth century that produced the richest crop of false Constantines" claiming to be heirs of the Byzantine throne.[14] A succession of pretenders has created false lineages, sometimes even having coins struck with their profiles, in grandiose efforts to establish their imperial merit.[15] These aspirants, along with pseudo-Stuarts or Tudors,[16] have been driven by "self-promotion" while claiming to be "obedient servants of their own dynastic sense of duty."[17] These "delusions of personal grandeur frequently cluster around episodes in history that have caught the popular imagination, especially those where there is a lingering sense of injustice, or at the least of unfinished business."[18]

In addition to titles, many lists appear to lift those who make them above the routine masses that don't. A few of these are Who's Who, Dean's List, Best Dressed, All-American, All-State, All-County, All-Star, Best Loved, "Entertainment Personalities—Where and When Born,"[19] "Widely Known Americans of the Present," and so on. There is also a plethora of halls of fame—more than three thousand in the United States alone, according to one estimate—although the large number would seem to dilute the amount of fame that might be conferred by membership in one.[20] There is, moreover, an abundance of honor societies.[21]

The astounding number of contests, tournaments, and pageants affords further opportunity for one to rise above his fellows. The obvious fear underlying many of these competitions is that if we don't search out the prettiest face or fastest feet, then that preeminence will be lost irretrievably. And our contests are not complete without a single winner. In fact, all sorts of mechanisms have been devised to prevent a plurality of winners—sudden-death overtimes, tie breakers, photo finishes, runoffs, extra innings, playoffs. It's somehow less satisfying to be forced to share the winner's circle and, moreover, the purpose of the contest (to distinguish as few people as possible) is hindered by multiple victors. Note the irony: We support thousands of contests so that all of us may be winners, yet we want each contest to coronate a single winner.

Seeking awards or credit for one's accomplishments is another way to reach for significance. In science and engineering, disputes have simmered over who deserved credit for important advances. One observer says, " 'The fact is that almost all of those firmly placed in the pantheon of science—Newton, Descartes, Leibnitz, Pascal, or Huyghens, Lister, Faraday, Laplace, or Davey—were caught up in passionate efforts to achieve priority and to have it publicly registered.' "[22] Witness the famous fight between Sir Isaac Newton and Gottfried Wilhelm Leibniz over who should receive credit for discovering the infinitesimal calculus. In reality, it seems that each arrived independently at the calculus at about the same time.[23]

Many people inflate or lie about their accomplishments in order to impress others. Some inflate their resumes, claiming awards or college degrees they don't have. Recent cases have included Ronald Zarella, the CEO of Bausch & Lomb, who falsely claimed to have earned an MBA from the New York University School of Business Administration, and George O'Leary, who lost his job as the newly hired football coach at the University of Notre Dame because he had falsely represented that he had a master's degree from New York University.[24]

Falsely claiming military service, even the Congressional Medal of Honor, has become so common that in 2005 Congress passed the Stolen Valor Act. This law made it a crime if one "falsely represents himself or herself, verbally or in writing, to have been awarded any decoration or medal authorized by Congress for the Armed Forces of the United States, any of the service medals or badges awarded to the members of such forces."[25]

Political offices, which number countless thousands just in the United States, give more opportunities for recognition. A veritable ocean of political offices is constantly being filled. Most of these election battles involve few substantive issues. They can best be described as battles of personalities. Their primary effect appears to be the provision of opportunities to pursue significance.

Record setting provides another popular way to acquire a position or document an accomplishment that no or few others have. Indeed, there is a record for every extreme of almost every conceivable category of human endeavor.

An early would-be record setter was John Ledyard, who in the 1700s strove to be the first person to walk around the world. Illuminating the human hunger for significance, he said, "There is an extensive field for the acquirement of honest fame. A blush of generous regret sits on my Cheek to hear of any Discovery there that I have not [had] part in."[26] Ledyard died of dysentery at the age of thirty-seven while trying to walk across Africa.[27]

Another record setter was Tito Gaona, who, according to *Sports Illustrated*, reigned in his day as the world's greatest living acrobat. He was the first person who was able consistently to do the triple somersault. Gaona vowed that before he retired he would do a quadruple somersault, which no one else had attempted. He said, "Someday I will do a quadruple and I will succeed and I will always be remembered."[28]

The *Guinness Book of World Records* contains records for everything from the length of fingernail growth, highest voice, longest hiccoughing attack, to the most body piercings.[29] Kenneth Crutchlow, who swam from Alcatraz Island to the shore of San Francisco Bay in near-freezing weather, said that he wanted to get his name in the *Guinness* book "even if it kills me."[30] A particularly sad attempt to set a record caused the death in 1996 of Jessica Dubroff, a seven-year-old girl. Her parents wanted her to set a record for the youngest person to fly a plane across the United States. She and her father both died when the plane crashed.[31]

Association with Something Bigger or More Permanent

In their analysis of the drive for fame, two British psychologists observe: "What we try to create . . . is some illusion of permanence. The desire for permanence drives people to carve their name on trees and rocks, just like the handprints on Hollywood Boulevard. We need to have an impact on life—to leave something behind us when we go."[32]

One way to satisfy that desire is by working as an inventor, designer, artist, or engineer to create or modify something beautiful or useful. Patent, trademark, and copyright laws permit one to keep the credit for one's developments and even to call them by one's own name.

A modern phenomenon is the practice of naming a star for a person. The International Astronomical Union officially names stars and other celestial bodies. But, blending capitalism with appeal to the human hunger for significance, several businesses now invite people, for a substantial fee, to name a star as a gift to, or in commemoration of, a person. These businesses issue a certificate, which can be framed for an extra charge.[33] An ad for one such business offers to name a "binary star system" that will "celebrate eternal love," for an additional fee of $17. This service even offers packages that include the launching into earth orbit by a "real aerospace company" of an "archive disk" that contains the name of one's star and a message. The website for this service warns, however, "no star-naming service changes the scientific designations of stars."[34] Indeed, the names sold by these star-naming services are purely fictitious and have no scientific or other validity.[35]

The year 2000 "Leave a Legacy Millennium" program at Epcot in Walt Disney World in Orlando furnishes another modern example. Participants paid a fee and signed a wordy contract under which Disney, a modern marketing juggernaut, agreed to photograph a guest(s) and affix the photograph, without the guest's name, to a location for twenty years. Disney was not obligated to repair or maintain the photograph. Under the contract, Disney could also, but was not obligated to, place the photograph on a website. Visitors to Epcot have been able to see thousands of these legacy photographs, each the size of a postage stamp (and unrecognizable), reproduced on metal plates fastened to granite steles. With a map, participants in the program have been able to locate their legacy photographs.[36]

Memory bricks are a similar phenomenon. Many charities and other organizations create gardens or walkways and, for a donation, inscribe the name of the donor or other specified person on the pavers. Appealing to the desire for significance, these monuments are a sure-fire way to raise funds. But almost no one notices the names on these bricks beneath their feet as they ply their daily routines.

Amassing property is another way to become a part of something larger and more permanent than one's self. A beautiful house surrounded by lush gardens and furnished with rare antiques and premium appliances attracts attention. The home may even become a museum after the owner's death, with strangers willing to pay a fee to tramp through his bedroom and wonder what he did in his spare time.

Also, a large estate enables one to ensure that his heirs will continue to act in reference to him after his death. One does this by making a will, setting up trusts, and buying life insurance. Wealth also enables one to perpetuate his name through funding a memorial scholarship or a university chair, or donating enough to have a room at the local hospital named for him. Psychiatrist Eric Berne notes, "Some philanthropists are more interested in competition than in benevolence:

'I gave more money (works of art, acres of land) than you did.' "[37] With the increase in the number of mega-rich and the sizes of their fortunes, there has been a corresponding increase in philanthropic competition.[38]

Many people are even bolder in their efforts to leave permanent reminders. The late President Lyndon B. Johnson affords an example. According to one commentator, "It is a curious footnote to history that long before he ran into trouble, Johnson had turned central Texas into a living monument to his heritage and his journey to the summit (the L.B.J. birthplace, the L.B.J. boyhood home, the L.B.J. state park, the L.B.J. ranch and more)."[39] In fact, Johnson's actions are not curious but are all too human. An ancient biblical example is furnished by Absalom, the son of King David: "Now Absalom in his lifetime had taken and set up for himself a pillar which is in the King's Valley, for he said, 'I have no son to preserve my name.' So he named the pillar after his own name, and it is called Absalom's monument to this day" (2 Samuel 18:18).

The non-famous leave their monuments, too. Before he died in 1947, John M. Davis, an orphan who had achieved a measure of wealth, spent all of his money ($250,000) on a memorial for himself and his wife in Hiawatha, Kansas. The memorial contained statues of Mr. and Mrs. Davis at various times in their lives. Because Davis spent all of his family's money on the memorial, the county had to pay for his funeral when he died. After a time, the memorial began sinking into the ground and, according to the secretary of Hiawatha's Mount Hope Cemetery, "No one seem[ed] to care."[40]

Graffiti and littering are the poor man's monuments. To some people it is almost unbearable to realize that, in the familiar places where they now live and eat and work and play, others will soon act in oblivion to their recent presence. So, they compulsively scribble their names on the bathroom wall or leave their gum stuck on the rail. Gwendolyn Brooks in her poem "Boy Breaking Glass" describes a child "whose broken window is a cry of art . . . 'I shall create! If not a note, a hole. If not an overture, a desecration.' "[41]

Many people try to foil their finitude by founding companies, organizations, or schools and calling them by their own names. Eponymy, or the practice of naming something for a person, is common in most literate human societies.[42] Absalom's monument and places named for President Johnson, which we just mentioned, are examples. More common are small businesses named after their owners or founders: Helen's Beauty Salon or Smith's Grocery.

Following this practice, the names of people are given to buildings, streets, parks, bridges, geographic areas,[43] and cities.[44] Names of people have also been given to comets (e.g., Halley's Comet for Sir Edmund Halley), tools (e.g., Phillips head screwdriver for Henry Phillips), medical devices (e.g., Foley catheter for Frederic Foley), medicines (e.g., the Salk vaccine for Jonas Salk),[45] formulas (e.g., the Pythagorean theorem for Pythagoras), physical phenomena (e.g., galvanization for Luigi Galvani), crimes (e.g., Ponzi scheme for Charles Ponzi; *Aktion Reinhard* for Reinhard Heydrich),[46] animals (e.g., spider Mastophora dizzydeani for baseball pitcher Dizzy Dean), plants (e.g., forsythia for William Forsyth), units and periods of time (e.g., August for Augustus Caesar and the Victorian era for Queen Victoria), articles of clothing (e.g., leotard for Jules Leótard), and even diseases (e.g., Alzheimer's disease for Alois Alzheimer).[47] Indeed, there are thousands of eponymous words in use today.[48]

J. Paul Getty (1892–1976) furnishes an example of one who sought to make a mark by both aggrandizement and eponymy. Getty was majority owner and president of the Getty Oil Company. When he died, he was the richest man in the world. In addition to naming his company for himself, he left the bulk of his fortune to the self-named J. Paul Getty Museum in California, making it the richest museum in the world. According to a close associate, Getty "wanted to make sure his name would be perpetuated as long as there was civilization."[49]

Robert Woodruff, the legendary president of The Coca-Cola Company, offers an intriguing study in the irresistible appeal of having things named after one. Woodruff built his company into an international conglomerate and Coca-Cola into the most recognized brand in the world. In the process, he became fabulously wealthy and used his riches to endow numerous organizations, most notably Emory University and various causes in Atlanta. Early in his philanthropic career, Woodruff donated money anonymously, acquiring the title

"Mr. Anonymous"—although, according to the mayor of Atlanta, even then his " 'identity. . . was the worst kept secret in Atlanta.' "[50] To the end of his life, Woodruff claimed as his animating creed: " 'There is no limit to what a man can do or where he can go if he doesn't mind who gets the credit.' "[51] But apparently Woodruff did mind: He wanted the credit. By the time he reached his later years, Woodruff had abandoned anonymity and agreed for the many organizations that benefited from his gifts to name a vast array of buildings, institutions, facilities, parks, and organizations for him and his family. As a result, his name and his family's names are some of the most prominently displayed ones to be found in any public venue in the world.[52]

There is often competition for naming privileges. Predictably, this competition has bid up the cost of first-choice naming opportunities. The *Wall Street Journal* has described this as "naming-rights inflation."[53] For example, New York real-estate developer Stephen Ross agreed in 2004 to donate $100 million to the University of Michigan Business School in return for an agreement to name the school in perpetuity for him. At the time, this was the largest gift ever made for naming rights to an American business school.[54] Generally, prominent institutions of higher learning have raised the price of naming not only for schools but also for scholarships, professorships, and buildings.[55]

However, there are hazards to branding. The Georgia Institute of Technology, for instance, removed the name of Thomas DuPree from its business school when he was unable to keep his $25 million pledge.[56] Seton Hall University in South Orange, New Jersey, has renamed Kozlowski Hall, which had been named for Dennis Kozlowski, the former CEO of Tyco International Ltd., who was convicted of securities fraud.[57]

Moreover, it is not unusual for an eponym to be diluted by multiple naming. For example, the Hartsfield Atlanta Airport for years has claimed the title of the world's busiest commercial airport. It was named for former Atlanta mayor William B. Hartsfield. Years later, when another Atlanta mayor, Maynard H. Jackson, died, the name was changed to Hartsfield-Jackson Atlanta International Airport. Hartsfield's family objected that this double-naming was "disrespectful."[58]

Even procreation may be a grasping for significance. Children continue their parents' name and can be expected to carry on many of their parents' values, beliefs, and a well-detailed memory of their parents' lives after they are gone. Children are a way to make one's self larger—two persons can become a family and maybe someday a dynasty. "I want my kids to surpass me," actor Kirk Douglas said, "because that's a form of immortality."[59] A seventeenth-century writer noted the irony that a parent seeks significance by having children while a military conqueror seeks it by destroying people: "A father leaves behind as many children as possible so as to perpetuate his name. A conqueror, to perpetuate his, exterminates as many people as possible."[60]

Association with Famous People and Things

For those who lack the resources or clout to have things named for them, a third primary course beckons. This method involves seeking significance by associating one's self in other ways with famous people or things, thereby absorbing glory from another. It may include something as mundane as buying products endorsed by a celebrity. "For some people, buying products associated with stars can serve as an emotional link between devotee and idol."[61] This is the poor man's eponymy.

Surveying the landscape of the famous, one could hardly choose a more promising target to which to attach one's self than Elvis Presley. And Joni Mabe of Cornelia, Georgia, has done just that. She has turned her family's boarding house into a museum of off-beat Elvis memorabilia. Her collection of more than thirty thousand artifacts includes a wart, a vial of sweat, and a toenail that she claims came from Elvis's body. Mabe also has hosted festivals devoted to Elvis.[62]

In our media-driven culture, it has become commonplace to form "para-social" or pseudo relationships with celebrities and sometimes even the roles they play. Instead of Elvis, others may identify with Rod Stewart or Barry Manilow.[63] "Fans often date what happens to them relative to what has happened to the star; they feel as if their lives and the star's have been woven together over the years."[64]

One scholar has identified a "Star Village," which consists of the approximately 100 persons who are immediately recognizable at any one time to most people. This village is the focus of an enormous amount of public attention and has increasingly replaced the real communities in which most persons lived before modern urbanization. Of course, the public participates in this illusory "community" only from a distance and through media conduits.[65]

One type of association with the famous has been called "basking in reflected glory" (BIRGing). This may occur when persons seek to boost their self-esteem by, for example, wearing clothing carrying the logos or names of successful sports teams or athletes.[66]

Many otherwise obscure persons have become famous by writing biographies or other works about famous persons. We have the ancient examples of Callisthenes, the historian of Alexander the Great, and Horace, the Roman poet who praised Augustus. Consider also James Boswell, who preserved his own name by writing the biography of Samuel Johnson. Another example is Irving Stone, who wrote an assortment of biographies and biographical novels of the famous including Michelangelo, Van Gogh, Clarence Darrow, and Abraham Lincoln.

Those who never write their idols' life stories may seek association with the famous by joining a fan club or even becoming a celebrity personal assistant. There is an Association of Celebrity Personal Assistants for those who seek careers as an "assistant to a star."[67]

Adulation of the famous can produce a strange transference in which fans imagine that they share the fame of their idols. The Bible opens a window on human behavior in the account of the men of Israel and those of Judah arguing over who should have brought the triumphant King David and his household over the Jordan (2 Samuel 19:41-43).

The Zapruder film of President John F. Kennedy's assassination furnishes another example of fame by association. Abraham Zapruder was an immigrant from the Ukraine working in the dressmaking business in Dallas, Texas. An admirer of Kennedy, he was filming the president's motorcade on November 22, 1963, when Kennedy was shot. Zapruder's twenty-six-second 8mm home movie, made with a Bell & Howell camera, became the primary record of the assassination and has been examined meticulously by the Warren Commission and many other investigators. As a result, Zapruder became famous, and he and his heirs were paid millions of dollars for rights to the film.[68]

A keen observer notes that even praise for famous persons may be an effort to share their fame. According to Tyler Cowen, "Many people praise Shakespeare not in an act of real homage but to display their own wisdom and demonstrate their excellent literary taste, hoping to capture a share of Shakespeare's renown."[69]

Impersonation furnishes another channel for the desire to associate with famous persons.[70] One website lists 320 Elvis impersonators around the world, including eager mimics in Australia,

Canada, France, the Philippines, and even Armenia.[71] Not surprisingly, there are organizations of professional Elvis impersonators. One such organization, based in the United Kingdom, mandates that its members adhere to a "Code of Professional Conduct" forbidding them from bringing "the name of Elvis Presley . . . into disrepute."[72]

Another common subject for impersonators is Abraham Lincoln. They too have an organization: the Association of Lincoln Presenters. It consists of 250 impersonators, most of whom try to dress and act like Lincoln, while a few impersonate his wife, Mary Todd Lincoln. As with the Elvis impersonators, they rent themselves out for events and special occasions.[73]

Moreover, we have impersonators of other almost-as-famous people, including various celebrities (Bob Hope, Barbara Streisand, Madonna, and now Sarah Palin). Under the tag "gigmasters," there is also a website listing these impersonators.[74]

Similar hunger to associate with the famous is evident in the veneration of places and objects that were frequented or used by people regarded as important. According to one observer, when we "memorialize . . . objects" it "offers us the hope that we pilgrims can absorb the influences of our heroes and live the rest of our lives having some share in their world."[75]

Thus, a bed that Franklin D. Roosevelt slept in or a desk that Napoleon used commands higher value than a better constructed bed or desk never used by a famous person. One recent auction brought $670 for a cigar half-smoked by Winston Churchill in 1950.[76] In another auction, a pair of Marilyn Monroe's prescription bottles fetched $18,750.[77] The same dynamic explains why "[e]very time you look at a house in Los Angeles, the real-estate agent will tell you that someone famous once lived there."[78]

A particularly robust industry has grown up around the collection of objects associated with Abraham Lincoln.[79] Many of the objects are held by museums and government agencies. But there are also numerous private collections. Louise Taper of Beverly Hills "owns the most spectacular collection of Lincolniana still in private hands."[80] One of her prize holdings is the chamber pot (i.e., toilet) that Lincoln used in the White House.[81] The mania in Lincoln collectibles includes "collecting catalogs of collectibles" and the emergence of a market in forged Lincoln signatures.

According to Andrew Ferguson's fascinating overview of the world of Lincoln, "Even more amazing, collectors who can't afford a Lincoln signature, and even some who can, have begun trading in forged Lincoln signatures—fakes, acknowledged and advertised as such, yet still somehow carrying (in the eyes of the willing collector) an ion of the original radiance. Bogus Lincoln letters can sell for thousands of dollars apiece, if they can be traced to one or another of a half dozen legendary forgers who flourished in the early twentieth century."[82] By possessing a forged Lincoln signature from a well-known forger, some persons apparently absorb a sense of importance.

Another example of the appeal of Lincoln for collectibles is a pen offered for sale by Fahrney's Pens, Inc. According to its marketers, this pen through "the most advanced technology" contains "a replication of [Abraham] Lincoln's DNA . . . crystallized and embedded in the amethyst stone on the crown of each limited edition pen." The price: $1,650.[83]

Of course, many collectors associate themselves with other historical figures. For example, Canadian businessman Ben Weider collected artifacts related to Napoleon. Weider assembled the largest privately held collection of such items. He endowed the eponymously named Ben Weider Eminent Scholar Chair in Napoleonic History at Florida State University, created The International Napoleonic Society (with himself as president), and wrote about his theory that Napoleon died from poisoning rather than the officially recognized cause of cancer.[84]

The tourist syndrome or desire to visit as many famous places as possible possesses many of us. Just to remind ourselves and others that we really did visit the Parthenon or Yellowstone National Park, we carve our names there, take a real or artificial piece of the place (souvenir), snap pictures, and/or sign the guest register. In our photo mania, we, as one observer has noted, are sometimes guilty of "sacrificing the present moment to make sure we get a good photo of it." And eventually the "event recedes in time and the photo becomes more and more the primary source for the memory."[85]

Too, we flock to points of excitement like fires, accidents, or parades, or try to remember where we were when the war ended or the president was shot. We seek to make these non-ordinary events part of our obscure lives.

Questions for Reflection

1. Why do you think people seek to be noticed and remembered by other persons?

2. Does it appear to you that most people think there is a God or some consciousness in the universe besides other humans who can notice and remember them? Elaborate on your answer.

3. What sorts of things do people do in an effort to be noticed and remembered by others?

4. What do you do in order to be noticed and remembered by others?

5. What titles, ranks, or listings in school, work, or politics have you achieved or sought? What was your motive?

6. Have you ever tried to set a record in a sport or some other activity? What was your motive?

7. Would you like to invent a new product or discover something for which you would receive credit and fame? Why?

8. Would obtaining a title, a superlative listing, setting a record, or inventing something affect your importance or worth as a person? Why or why not?

9. Have you ever envied those who have obtained lofty titles, listings, or records? Have you ever envied those who have received credit for inventing or discovering something? Why do you think you feel that way?

10. Have you ever paid to have your name or the name of a family member carved onto a memory brick or monument? Would you like for a monument to honor you either now or after you die? What is or would be your motive?

11. Would you like to have a place—such as a building, road, or even lake or mountain—named for you? Why or why not?

12. Would having something named for you affect your importance or worth as a person? How?

3. Efforts at Significance, Part Two

In E-Sagil . . . let my name be ever repeated.
—Code of Hammurabi (ca. 2250 BC)

I'm as important as the Start of WWI just need the little opening & a second of time.
—Arthur Bremer (while seeking to assassinate a public official)[1]

A s we have seen, individuals do many things to seek significance. We looked at attempts to reach positions or accomplishments that set us apart from others by acquiring titles or setting records. In addition, we saw how we try to attach ourselves to things that seem bigger or more permanent than we by seeking credit for inventions or having places or things named for us. Moreover, we have explored efforts to associate with famous people and things.

But these are not the only ways in which we try to satisfy our need to be known, appreciated, influential, and remembered. Another way we do this is by attempting to record and preserve our lives and histories. Some people also use crime to attract attention to themselves. Finally, others pursue an assortment of miscellaneous actions.

Preserving One's Personal Life, Group History, and Culture

Beyond the ways reviewed in the last chapter in which persons seek significance, another general means is through preserving our personal lives, group histories, and culture. As to our personal lives, we record our thoughts and actions in diaries and journals, fearing them eternally lost otherwise; write our memoirs; collect trophies, plaques, certificates, diplomas; keep scrapbooks of memorabilia; save old letters and cards; observe birthdays and anniversaries; bronze our baby shoes; keep our family records up to date; ferret out our ancestry; freeze part of the wedding cake; record our ideas in books and articles; try to say in a treatise or scholarly work everything there is to say on a subject; talk about ourselves in venues such as press conferences; and let others know what we are doing through cards, letters, phone-calls, emails, and now tweets.

Addressing our urge to preserve, entrepreneurs have started businesses that convert family home movies to "permanent" media like DVDs.[2] Some of these businesses also offer to organize and duplicate the DVDs, making them suitable for gifts.

These urges are reflected, not only in the standard attic clutter and memorabilia madness that afflict us all, but also in recent trends of enhanced scrapbook techniques and the construction of new mini-warehouse storage facilities.

Robert Shields was an elderly retired minister and teacher who lived in Dayton, Washington. For twenty-five years, he spent four hours each day writing a minute-by-minute diary of all of his activities. His diary, which is believed to be the world's longest, was 37.5 million words long and filled ninety-four cartons when he died. Following are examples of entries in his diary:

July 25, 1993
7 am: I cleaned out the tub and scraped my feet with my fingernails to remove layers of dead skin.
7.05 am: Passed a large, firm stool, and a pint of urine. Used five sheets of paper.

April 18, 1994
6.30-6.35: I put in the oven two Stouffer's macaroni and cheese at 350°.
6.35-6.50: I was at the keyboard of the IBM Wheelwriter making entries for the diary.
6.50-7.30: I ate the Stouffer's macaroni and cheese and Cornelia ate the other one. Grace decided she didn't want one.
7.30-7.35: We changed the light over the back stoop since the bulb had burnt out.

August 13, 1995
8.45 am: I shaved twice with the Gillette Sensorblade [and] shaved my neck behind both ears, and crossways of my cheeks, too.

Shields recorded his vital signs at various times every day, the outside temperature, every conversation he had, every piece of mail he received. He even attached materials to his diary such as labels from food he ate or nasal hairs collected from his personal hygiene. Shields admitted that, because he was so consumed with maintaining his diary, he never had time to edit or read it. According to a National Public Radio report, Shields spent his life savings of $100,000 to endow the Washington State University Library, which agreed in turn to house his diary.[3]

Some people resort to webcams that beam their most intimate and trivial activities around the world 24/7 on the Internet.[4] For those only slightly more modest, the popular website YouTube is available for uploading selections of one's own pedestrian image and voice to the Internet, alongside those of the truly famous.

Individual humans are obviously transient, and their environment has long served to add supposed permanence to their existence. But when the environment changes faster than people do, they feel insecure. This helps explain why some have opposed the building boom in Paris, for example.[5] Alvin Toffler's *Future Shock* explores the untoward psychological effects of rapid change.[6] The accelerating rate of change makes each of us more painfully aware of our minute finitude in a gigantic universe.

Much effort also goes into preserving the history and culture that surrounds us. The fear of losing the past is especially prevalent in places like Italy, for example, which contains so much history that it cannot be given proper care—some thirty thousand historic churches, sixty thousand historic religious edifices, two hundred state museums, and many more regional and local museums. Robert Hughes has said, "All this must be preserved."[7]

Although we may not personally be responsible for the first instance of a human accomplishment, we can still seek to preserve our history and culture by discovering and recording all kinds of firsts. Books like *The Book of Firsts*[8] and *Famous First Facts*[9] record things like the first lion tamer, the first dry-cleaner, and the inventor of the potato chip.

Like squirrels preparing for winter we store away events in newspapers, magazines, encyclopedias, libraries, archives, recordings, museums, almanacs, time capsules, annuals, statistics, and halls of fame. The technological developments of printing, voice recording, photography, photocopying, microfilm, digitizing, and electronic storage of data have facilitated the preservation of history that would otherwise apparently be lost. Appropriately then, the expressed goal of Google Inc. is to digitize all human knowledge.[10]

But even digitization creates its own problems. Who is going to organize, preserve, and provide accessibility for the increasingly large mountains of electronic data? According to *The Wall Street Journal*, "Computer users worldwide generate enough digital data every 15 minutes to fill the U.S. Library of Congress."[11] One scientist says, "The data is doubling every year."[12] An example is data collected by telescopes and observatories. Dr. Sayeed Choudhoury, a digital curator at Johns Hopkins University, reports that the Sloan Digital Sky

Survey, which uses a telescope in New Mexico, gathered more data in its first two days than in all the previous history of astronomy, some 140 terabytes of digital data.[13] "Our ability to collect data now outstrips our ability to maintain it for the long run," says William Michener of the University of New Mexico.[14] And as all computer users who have experienced the crash of a hard drive know, digital information can be fragile. It can also become inaccessible due to changes in technology and formatting.[15]

Technology should make it easier to preserve in the future. The bodies of many people, including famed baseball hitter Ted Williams,[16] have already been frozen in a process called cryonics. Some even attempt to leave vast sums of money to themselves in so-called revival trusts, which they could reclaim if they were brought back to life in the future.[17]

And science is always at work on prolonging human life. Some scientists foresee the possibility that a person's personality and knowledge could be programmed into a computer that will not die. Russian multimillionaire Dmitry Itskov sponsors and funds the "2045 Initiative," which by the year for which it is named seeks to do just that. The project "envisions the mass production of lifelike, low-cost avatars that can be uploaded with the contents of a human brain."[18]

Crime and Destructive Behavior

Crime and destructive behavior, because they also offer attention, unfortunately furnish another main avenue for souls in search of significance. Those who follow this path might prefer to be the next George Washington, but with that route appearing to be closed, they settle for being another John Dillinger. British historian Fred Inglis comments, "Notoriety will do for those who cannot win fame well."[19] There seems to be unlimited room for new villains, but not much for new heroes.

An early instance was the burning by Herostratos in 356 BC of the great temple of Artemis at Ephesus, considered one of the seven wonders of the ancient world. According to classical sources, he did so to secure immortal fame.[20] The outraged Ephesians banned the mention of his name, but, demonstrating the dividends sometimes paid for destructive conduct, Herostratos is the only Ephesian from his era whose name remains known. The names of the builders of the temple, its priests, and the city magistrates have been lost to history.[21]

Much motiveless arson and vandalism can be explained as an attempt to leave one's mark, to let others know that he once passed this way. Even works of art, among them the Mona Lisa and the Pieta, have been attacked by vandals. It is unlikely that the perpetrators of these crimes were driven by their distaste for daVinci's and Michelangelo's artistic styles. Rather, they apparently sought in a twisted way to soak up some of the fame of the objects and their creators.

Arson, when committed by one who holds a casualty insurance policy, is often intended to collect insurance benefits. Yet a substantial amount of arson roots in the desire for significance. For example, in 2005 Joseph Stone torched a Pittsfield, Massachusetts, apartment building where he lived and worked as a maintenance man. After setting the blaze, Stone rescued several tenants from the fire and was hailed as a hero. Under police questioning, Stone admitted, however, that he set the fire and rescued the tenants because, as summarized at trial by an assistant district attorney, he "wanted to be noticed, he wanted to be heard, he wanted to be known."[22]

More violent crimes, too, may at bottom be attempts toward significance.[23] Academic researchers Jean Twenge and Keith Campbell have commented on the modern "trend toward seeking fame by hurting—or even killing—someone else."[24] Leo Braudy adds, "In a world preoccupied with names, faces, and voices, fame promises acceptability, even if one commits the most heinous crime, because thereby people will finally know who you are, and you will be saved from the living death of being unknown."[25]

Robert Hawkins was a nineteen-year-old teenager who spent years in treatment centers, group homes, and foster care. In December 2007, he was unemployed, had been rejected by his family and girlfriend, and had lost his job at McDonald's. Hawkins walked into an

Omaha shopping mall, killed eight persons, and wounded five others with an AK-47 rifle, which he then turned on himself. Hawkins left a suicide note stating: "I'm going to be f------ famous." He now has his own Wikipedia page.[26]

Assassination and assassination attempts directed at public figures in the United States have usually been driven not by political motives but by the thirst "to achieve notoriety/fame."[27] Arthur Bremer, who shot Alabama Governor George Wallace as he campaigned for president in Maryland in May 1972, is a revealing example. Bremer was a twenty-one-year-old unemployed busboy who had no friends. "Hey World! Come Here I wanna talk to you!" he said in the diary he kept before the shooting.[28]

Bremer's desperate struggle to make a mark reverberates in this diary entry: "I'm as important as the Start of WWI just need the little opening & a second of time."[29] Before Bremer settled on shooting Wallace, he stalked President Richard Nixon while Nixon was on a state visit to Canada. Six times, according to Bremer's diary, Nixon passed by at too great a distance or speed for him to shoot. After watching Nixon go by for the sixth time—now in a bulletproof limousine—Bremer, performing a cold cost-benefit calculation, wrote, "I wasn't sure my flat tipped .38's would go through the bulletproof glass. Didn't want to get enprisoned [sic] or killed in an unsuccessful attempt. To have absolutely nothing to show—I couldn't take that chance."[30] The pervasive motive behind all efforts at significance—to alter or change the world to show that one has been here—reveals itself in this entry also made after Bremer missed Nixon that sixth time: "All my efforts & nothing changed. Just another god Damn failure."[31]

Having missed Nixon, Bremer looked around for another apparently important person whom he could kill and whose importance or fame thereby absorb. He reluctantly settled on Wallace, whom he did not consider famous enough to bring him the attention that he sought. Bremer's diary shows his dissatisfaction at making Wallace a target:

> I won't even rate a T.V. enterobtion [sic] in Russia or Europe when the news breaks—they never heard of Wallace. If something big in Nam [Viet Nam] flares up I'll end up at the bottom of the 1st page in America. The editors will say—"Wallace dead? Who cares." He won't get more than 3 minutes on network T.V. news.[32]

Although Bremer failed to kill Wallace, he paralyzed the governor and got the attention he sought. What he predicted for his diary—"This will be one of the most closely read papers since the Scrolls in those caves"[33]—came true. It was published in both *Harper's Magazine* and book form.

The motive of the assassin of President John Kennedy was apparently not truly political either. Lee Harvey Oswald was small in stature, a high school dropout, ridiculed and thrown out of the Marines, talentless, friendless, abused and rejected by his wife, and sexually impotent.[34] One of Oswald's squad mates in the Marines said Oswald wanted to do something that people would talk about in ten thousand years.[35] Efforts have been made to attribute a political motive to him, but it appears that Oswald's actions fundamentally represented a desperate cry for significance. Denying that Oswald's motives were political, Robert Oswald, the brother of the assassin, said: "He's looking for attention, always looking for attention that he never got at home unfortunately."[36]

Mark David Chapman shot and killed former Beatle John Lennon on a Manhattan sidewalk on December 8, 1980. Chapman, who claimed to be a Beatles fan and obtained Lennon's autograph the same day he shot Lennon, has justified the murder by his desire for attention: "I was an acute nobody. I had to usurp someone else's importance, someone else's success. I was 'Mr. Nobody' until I killed the biggest Somebody on earth."[37] At his 2006 parole hearing, he stated: "The result would be that I would be famous, the result would be that my life would change and I would receive a tremendous amount of attention, which I did receive . . . . I was looking for reasons to vent all that anger and confusion and low self-esteem."[38]

Assassination for publicity is not, of course, limited to the United States or the modern era. According to Roman historian Valerius Maximus, Pausanias assassinated Philip of Macedon in 336 BC in order "to be remembered forever."[39] In 1898, former Italian soldier Luigi Lucheni assassinated Empress Elisabeth of Austria while she was

47

visiting in Geneva. Lucheni, who felt that his life had been miserable, told his roommate "that he would like to kill a person of importance who was well known, so that the newspapers would talk of the event."[40]

Mass murderers are usually unsuccessful, friendless loners. Their motivation in slaughtering as many people as possible is often to compensate, in some twisted way, for their frustrations and lack of success. Cho Seung-hui, who killed thirty-two persons and then himself (and wounded twenty-five others) on the campus of Virginia Tech in 2007, furnishes an example. He interrupted his murderous spree long enough to run to a nearby post office and mail a ranting prerecorded video and manifesto to NBC News in New York before resuming his slaughter.[41] Indeed, Cho received the publicity he sought. More than two years after his rampage, one Internet search of the name of this previously unknown twenty-three-year-old, who succeeded at nothing, produced over 2,500,000 hits on www.google.com (more than some US presidents), including a lengthy Wikipedia article.[42] Expressing a megalomanic desire for significance, Cho ranted in the DVD he sent to NBC: "I die like Jesus Christ to inspire generations of the weak and the defenceless [sic] people."[43]

Further illustrating the desire for significance that fuels some crimes, there are numerous examples of criminals who go undetected (which one would think is the goal of all criminals) but, unhappy with their lack of attention, reach out for publicity—thus enabling the police to solve their crimes. Although conscience may be a factor, it appears that the desire for recognition or significance plays a much larger role for some of these criminals. Albert De Salvo, the self-confessed Boston Strangler who murdered thirteen women in the early 1960s, killed for the same reason that Bremer shot Wallace. De Salvo's wife recalled of her husband, "He always wanted to be important." And De Salvo once admitted, "I'm nothing in this life . . . . But I want to be something."[44] De Salvo confessed to these murders which had baffled police. It is unlikely that he ever would have been caught had he not confessed.[45]

Over numerous years, Dennis Rader killed as many as thirteen people in Wichita, Kansas. This unlikely killer was a municipal code enforcement supervisor, married, father of two, Boy Scout leader, and president of the council at his Lutheran church. His crimes remained unsolved for more than thirty years. During his extended crime spree, Rader sent rambling letters to the media, including one in which he gave himself the nickname BTK, standing for Bind, Torture, Kill—reflecting the methods by which he slaughtered his victims. In another letter, he complained, "How many times do I have to kill before I get my name in the paper or some national attention." Rader directed to the media and police numerous other taunting letters and items from victims' bodies. His efforts to get "credit" for his "work" eventually created the break that police needed to arrest and charge Rader.[46]

Many people even make bogus confessions to crimes they did not commit. More than two hundred people confessed in 1932 to the kidnapping and murder of the infant son of famed aviator Charles Lindbergh. Ironically, the person who was ultimately convicted, Bruno Hauptmann, maintained his innocence until he was executed.[47] Within a few years of her murder in 1966, nineteen false confessions were made to the murder of Valerie Percy, the twenty-one-year-old daughter of then-Senator Charles H. Percy of Illinois. The murder remains unsolved.[48] The widely publicized false confession by John Mark Karr to the sensational murder of child beauty queen JonBenet Ramsey in Boulder, Colorado, at Christmas 1996 stands as another graphic example of this phenomenon.[49]

Miscellaneous Actions

Finally, a miscellany of unlikely actions sometimes boil down to the quest for significance. Religious activities may, for example, be motivated by the desire for attention. Among the ways that the scribes and Pharisees would "do all their deeds to be noticed by men" (Matthew 23:5)—and for which Jesus criticized them—were displaying their long robes (Mark 12:38) and tassels (Matthew 23:5), loving the front seats in the synagogues and places of honor at banquets (Luke 1:43; Matthew 23:1-3,5,6), praying long and publicly in order to be seen by others (Matthew 6:5-7, 23:14 Mark 12:38,40; Luke 18:9-14), making sure their fasting was noticed by men (Matthew 6:16-18), sounding a trumpet when they gave alms

(Matthew 6:2-4), loving high-sounding titles and respectful greetings (Matthew 23:1-3, 5-10), and even showing off their knowledge of Scripture (Matthew 23:5).

Another unlikely place to find this longing for significance at work is in misfortunes. The idea is that "my misfortunes are better than yours."[50] One may brag about the number of accidents, diseases, wars, and fights he has survived. Eric Berne adds:

> As a game, "Ain't It Awful" finds its most dramatic expression in polysurgery addicts, and their transactions illustrate its characteristics. These are doctor-shoppers, people who actively seek surgery even in the face of sound medical opposition. The experience itself, the hospitalization and surgery, brings its own advantages. . . . The internal social advantages come from medical and nursing staff, and from other patients. After the patient's discharge the external social advantages are gained by provoking sympathy and awe.[51]

Berne also notes that one may keep an illness secret in order to impress others with his fortitude when it finally becomes known.[52] In Albert Camus's *The Plague*, Cottard takes pride that he had the plague first and that he survived it:

> Thus Cottard (if we may trust Tarrou's diagnosis) had good grounds for viewing the symptoms of mental confusion and distress in those around him with an understanding and an indulgent satisfaction that might have found expression in the remark: "Prate away, my friends—but I had it first."[53]

51

Substance abuse, when dissected, may often turn out to be a strategy to evoke sympathy and/or anger. Berne says, "The transactional object of drinking, aside from the personal pleasures it brings is to set up a situation where the child can be severely scolded not only by the internal parent but by any parental figures in the environment who are interested enough to oblige."[54]

Aggressive behavior, even when it falls short of criminal conduct, may also be a demand for attention. Ashley Montagu explains: "Hostility, aggressiveness, and 'bad' behavior are simply techniques for securing love, for compelling the attention of those who have refused it."[55]

The Internet, "reality" television shows, and other modern media offer novel opportunities to seek fame. *The Wall Street Journal* summarizes that "the Internet and reality television—and the lifestyle trends they have helped to cultivate this decade—have added a number of paths to publicity, if not prominence."[56] The proliferation of reality television shows offers the possibility of "making television celebrities out of ordinary people."[57] A website that provides a pathway for those seeking to appear in reality programming is www.beonscreen.com.[58]

Another website, which offers mock fame, is www.celeb 4aday.com. Depending on the product a customer purchases (such as the "MegaStar Package"), the company that runs the website will, for a hefty fee, hire photo-snapping paparazzi who follow a customer while shouting her name and vying for her attention, a publicist, a limo, and a bodyguard to treat the customer like a celebrity for up to two hours. The customer even receives a mocked-up celebrity tabloid with her picture on the cover. A company motto assures us that "the everyday person deserves the attention as much, if not more, than the real celebrities."[59]

Using Facebook and other social media, one can share personal information, photos, and an endless stream of superficial messages with more people than was ever possible before the Internet. Some call this practice an aspect of the Web 2.0. Social media create the illusion of personal interaction or friendships. Indeed, Facebook uses the term "friend" to refer to those with whom one is "connected" over the Internet. Younger people especially, who are more likely to use social media sites, compete among themselves over who has the most Facebook "friends."[60] Candice Kelsey observes, "Many of the friending exchanges that take place reek of social climbing, posturing, self-aggrandizement, or accumulation. Rarely do two people friend each other out of a sincere desire to relate, grow in intimacy, and strengthen a bond."[61]

One enterprising soul has written "How to Become Famous Online Without Spending a Dime."[62] Another website, www.IWannaBe Famous.com, will post your entries if you "send . . . your photo today and tell . . . why you wanna be famous!"[63] Now the website www.twitter.com has taken the world by storm, allowing common persons to follow minute by minute the moves and thoughts of the famous, and perhaps themselves become famous or gain a following of their own.

Some people resort to alterations in their appearances in order to attract attention. Charles Derber, a sociologist at Boston College who has studied the human appetite for attention, notes the "throngs of both boys and girls [who] exhibit green or orange hair and pierced noses, navels, or tongues, in the multiple forms of body mutilation and punk fashion that are among the most brazen means of attracting attention in teen culture."[64]

Finally, many seemingly thoughtless actions may root in the desire for significance—as those of the swaggering Dostoyevsky character who makes "a disgusting chatter with his sword."[65] Other examples of making "a presentation of ourselves to others"[66] may be clearing one's throat repeatedly when forced to sit next to one who appears inferior, standing up amid a seated group, and vying with others to dominate a question-and-answer session. Indeed, "there is a rush that comes with commanding everyone's attention" even by "telling a good story at a cocktail party."[67] In the words of Leo Braudy, "daily life" may be "perceived in great part as a constant performance before an audience of others."[68]

What are the effects of our efforts to receive significance or attention from other people? Let's turn to that question next.

Questions for Reflection

1. Do you know people whom seem to be driven to record and preserve all of their thoughts and activities? How have you seen people pursue this?

2. Do you ever feel that your thoughts and activities will be forgotten and lost if you don't record and preserve them? What have you done in reaction to this feeling?

3. Do you ever feel compelled to uncover and preserve your genealogy or family history? Do you pursue this as an interesting hobby or because you fear that your ancestors will be forgotten if you don't preserve their memories?

4. Have you ever seen television shows about people who hate to throw things anyway and as a result live in a squalid ocean of junk? Some may do this because of a mental disorder, but do you think others do this because they feel that they must preserve all the pieces of their lives?

5. What do you think of the trend of wealthy persons leaving revival trusts with funds that might be used in the future to bring them back to life and cure previously incurable diseases or injuries? Why would someone do this?

6. Can you think of any unusual ways in which people try to preserve their personal lives, group history, and culture? What are some of those ways?

7. Have you seen any examples of people engaging in destructive behavior in order to attract attention?

8. When you pray out loud in public, do you find yourself choosing your words or listening to the tone of your voice in order to sound good to other people? If so, why do you think this happens?

9. When you sing hymns or praise songs are you preoccupied with whether other persons are listening and seem impressed by your voice? Does this affect your worship?

10. Are there other ways that you find yourself practicing your faith in order to impress other people? If so, what are those ways?

11. Can you think of any instances when people seem to be talking about their illnesses or injuries in order to attract attention?

4. Negative Effects of the Competition for Significance

And there arose also a dispute among [the disciples] as to which one of them was regarded to be the greatest.
—Luke 22:24

"Pray, what are you laughing at?" inquired the Rocket, "I am not laughing."

"I am laughing because I am happy," replied the Cracker.

"That is a very selfish reason," said the Rocket angrily. "What right have you to be happy? You should be thinking about others. In fact, you should be thinking about me. I am always thinking about myself, and I expect everybody else to do the same."
—Oscar Wilde, "The Remarkable Rocket"[1]

As we have seen, crime and destructive behavior provide a negative way to pursue significance. But what effects result from other efforts to attain significance?

The desire for significance inevitably places people into conflict with each other. As the population multiplies, the individual's importance seems to diminish and others are frequently viewed as threats or competitors to one's significance. Sociologist Charles Derber has recognized "that the competition for attention is one of the key contests of social life" and that this "attention plays a role in social interaction as does money in the economy; people hunger for it and suffer terribly from its deprivation."[2] Derber adds that "routine forms of attention-seeking . . . now infect much of our workplace or family interaction and have a deep and sometimes debilitating effect on our everyday lives."[3] He describes the proliferation of practices like those of the characters on the hit television show *Seinfeld* who are "so comically absorbed with talking about and promoting themselves that they could not form meaningful relationships." Derber calls this "conversational narcissism."[4]

Other observers describe an epidemic of narcissism in modern society. This is fed by the tabloid press, celebrity magazines and television shows, and our now constant companion called the Internet. Social media sites are leading the way. As mentioned earlier, Facebook and MySpace users who compare and rate themselves by the number of "friends" or "contacts" they have are prime examples.[5] A recent book on narcissism notes: "Having more friends is a status symbol, and it's embarrassing to only have five friends on MySpace or Facebook."[6]

Envy emerges as a large consequence to this struggle. Gore Vidal sums up our feelings: "Whenever a friend succeeds, a little something in me dies." Solomon underscores: "[E]very labor and every skill which is done is the result of rivalry between a man and his neighbor." (Ecclesiastes 4:4).

Famous persons—always trailed by paparazzi and constantly bathed in the glare of camera lights—are envied by those who don't attract such attention. As Walter Winchell said, "The way to become famous fast is to throw a brick at someone who is famous."[7] This served as the fundamental motive of Herostratos, who burned the ancient temple of Artemis at Ephesus, and other destructive fame seekers, such as assassins of prominent persons. They seek to "absorb the celebrity" of their target, whether a person or a thing.[8]

Moreover, many professional entertainers are jealous of their popularity—they cannot bear to be upstaged. Al Jolson, for example, would not permit any other acts on his Sunday concert bills to please the audience. According to his biographer, "He once had a team of performing elephants fired because he thought the audience liked them too much."[9] Muhammad Ali kept fighting at the risk of injury because he was, according to one observer, "a junkie for fame." He could not resist hearing himself announced as "the undisputed heavyweight champion of the world."[10]

The same attitudes prevailed in biblical times. King Saul envied David when the women sang after David's victory over Goliath, "Saul has slain his thousands, and David his ten thousands" (1 Samuel 18:7-9).

What has been called "the sideways glance of envy" causes one to criticize others, to take pleasure in their downfall, or to pass them off as "wimps," "dinky," "losers," or "old fashioned." Proverbs 14:30

describes the corrosive effects of envy as "rottenness to the bones" (NKJV). This explains Jesus' warning in the Sermon on the Mount against our tendency to say that others are "good-for-nothing" or "Raca," which is a way of murdering or destroying people. (Matthew 5:21-22). Envy may even lead to violence such as tearing down others' monuments. Witness the stories of Amenhotep and other Egyptian pharaohs who erased the names of others (even their own fathers') from inscriptions and substituted their own.[11]

Another negative effect is that the clamor for attention and adulation can obscure and cause the neglect of more worthy and necessary pursuits. For example, the modern US presidency, with the now-standard presidential library and the constant glare of electronic media, has seemingly evolved into an unabashed perpetual pursuit of a better legacy rather than a drive for better policies. Derber describes President Bill Clinton in his "scandal-plagued second term" as "sucking in the adulation like an asthmatic gasping for oxygen" and "turning the Presidency into an eternal campaign for public attention and acclaim."[12] According to Derber, the appetite for attention threatens democracy and community: "Whenever the pursuit of attention turns into a national obsession, there lurks the danger of breakdown of social life based on the emotional unavailability of each of us to one another."[13]

In addition to bringing harassment by paparazzi, celebrity often creates other negative effects. This includes bad marriages, poor emotional health, drug and alcohol abuse, suicide, and other dysfunctions.[14]

Apart from their negative consequences, are our efforts to attain significance by attracting human attention truly successful and satisfying? Let's explore this question next.

Questions for Reflection

1. How does competition for attention and fame lead to conflict among people?

2. Can you think of any instances of people becoming angry and resentful over the attention given others? What are some examples.

3. Have you ever had a good idea or accomplished something and seen another person receive credit for it? How did that make you feel?

4. How do you feel when others receive fame and attention?

5. It is often said that there is no limit to what a person can accomplish if he does not care who receives the credit. But do we in fact care who gets the credit?

6. How do you feel when persons you know receive public acknowledgment?

7. Do you ever have a desperate feeling that your time is running out and you must make a mark or leave a legacy before you die? What would you consider a satisfactory legacy?

5. Human Efforts Fail to Achieve Significance

For there is no lasting remembrance of the wise man as with
the fool, inasmuch as in the coming days all will be forgotten
And how the wise man and the fool alike die!
                                        —Ecclesiastes 2:16

Their inner thought is that their houses are forever,
And their dwelling places to all generations;
They have called their lands after their own names.
But man in his pomp will not endure;
he is like the beasts that perish. . . .
Do not be afraid when a man becomes rich,
When the glory of his house is increased;
For when he dies he will carry nothing away;
His glory will not descend after him.
Though while he lives he congratulates himself—
And though men praise you when you do well for yourself—
He shall go to the generation of his fathers;
They will never see the light.
                                        —Psalm 49:11-12, 16-19

Do these efforts to reach significance succeed? Is it possible by one's efforts to satisfy the longing for significance?

It is painfully clear that, even after all our posing and desperate screams for someone to notice us, we still seem dreadfully small and ignored. Our "days are like grass" or a flower that blooms in the morning and dies in the afternoon. But what hurts worse is that this transient flower is one whose "place acknowledges it no longer" after it is gone (Psalm 103:14-16). In other words, even in the locations that we commonly visit things continue, once we are gone, as if we had never even been there at all. This absence of any mark or legacy seems even more cruel than the transience.

One case study on the futility of the quest for individual human significance is the Old Testament story of Haman, a high government minister in ancient Persia. When Mordecai, a Jewish exile who was in captivity, failed to acknowledge his importance, Haman reacted in a way typical of all of us. He bragged about his position, possessions, and family.

> [B]ut when Haman saw Mordecai in the king's gate, and that he did not stand up or tremble before him, Haman was filled with anger against Mordecai. Haman . . . sent for his friends and his wife Zeresh. Then Haman recounted to them the glory of his riches, and the number of his sons, and every instance where the king had magnified him, and how he had promoted him above the princes and servants of the king.
> Haman also said, "Even Esther the queen let no one but me come with the king to the banquet which she had prepared; and tomorrow also I am invited by her with the king."

After listing all of his accomplishments and honors, Haman spoke for all of us (those with human prestige and those without) in saying: "Yet all of this does not satisfy me" (Esther 5:9-13).

A modern parallel is novelist Tom Wolfe's character, Charlie Croker, in *A Man in Full*. Faced with declining health and financial reversals, Croker surveys his possessions in the prestigious Atlanta neighborhood of Buckhead and recognizes their futility:

> He felt enormously sorry for himself . . . an old man being trundled in a wheelchair to a bed in his library. A sorry old man letting his eyes wander helplessly over his worldly goods . . . And what nonsense it all was! How vain and petty it all was, all this exulting over . . . things! One day—soon enough!—we'll all be gone, and there'll be people rooting through all this . . . stuff . . . like maggots . . . What are antiques, after all, but objects other maggots went over before you? And what is this whole house . . . in the sacred Buckhead . . . but a place he was renting until the next group of renters, as desperate to live in Buckhead as he was, took over.[1]

The significance that we desire deep inside is total—that we be known exhaustively everywhere. Each of us feels that even our most fleeting and most trivial thoughts and actions are somehow important. But the first roadblock to total significance is this: If people are the only conscious and sentient beings in the universe, I'm already left out of most history when I am born because the vast majority of people who have walked the earth already lived and died before I arrived.

Moreover, we cannot even attain a satisfactory significance among our contemporaries. A crippling problem is that no person is even completely aware of himself and his history. We are not really sure what we think, and we forget our thoughts and actions that we do apprehend. For example, I probably remember very little of what I did last Friday and almost nothing that I did one year ago today. How many movies have you seen, books and newspapers have you read, places have you visited, people have you met of which you have no recollection and your association with which is nowhere recorded or remembered? A person can't even tell a spouse everything he or she did that day when coming home for dinner. And old age decimates what memories we do retain.

Are we any better at recording what we do? No one can record and preserve even what little he knows about himself. No diary is large enough, and no diarist has time enough to detail everything about himself—even Robert Shields who kept the world's largest diary (see chap. 3). The volume of events is too immense and their succession too swift.

The opportunities for fame may now seem unlimited, with the historical march of expanding ways to record and promote one's words, image, and deeds. First there was only memory and oral transmission. Then came writing, engraving, sculpture, portraiture, printing, and photography, and now instant mass electronic communications over the Internet.[2] Yet there lurk insurmountable limits. Fame can be subdivided only so far before it evaporates. In other words, how much public attention is there to pass around? Before the modern era the memories of only a few famous gods and persons endured over time, but now fame has been "thinned out in a million fleeting images on the evening news."[3]

This explosion of fame has also tilted the scales away from "the famous names of history, such as politicians, inventors or explorers" and in favor of celebrities from the world of entertainment.[4] If, as Andy Warhol said, everyone will be famous for fifteen minutes, then really no one is famous. Assuming that fifteen minutes is all you get, then by definition you are forgotten when your fifteen minutes expire and it's someone else's turn.

The achievement of significance is also undermined by another problem. Many of the titles and rankings we bestow on people are probably inaccurate. There is no way to judge accurately who is the greatest (or who are the ten greatest) baseball players or athletes of another sport. The presumed conclusiveness of sport is an illusion. For example, in identifying the greatest tennis player of all time, should the change in racket composition be considered in order to be fair to those who played with the old wooden rackets, should professionals and amateurs be lumped together, should the age at which a player retired be considered, should injuries be taken into account, should the length of productive play be considered, should major tournament wins be decisive?[5] The same question could be asked about other fields of endeavor. How can it be decided who are the best one hundred heart surgeons in the United States, the best one hundred attorneys in California, the best public speakers, the best tenor of all time?

One example of the failure of history accurately to attribute priority or success is manned flight. German immigrant Gustave Whitehead is now recognized as having made manned flights well before Wilbur and Orville Wright. But Whitehead has to this day never received the recognition in aviation history and popular culture that the Wrights have received.[6]

If we can't know ourselves exhaustively, we cannot be known completely by other persons. One person can never begin to know even superficially all the people presently living. It would take thousands of years to spend a mere one minute with each of the world's presently living seven billion people.[7] And, even if this were possible, what could be learned in one minute and remembered?

Putting aside the problem of communicating information about oneself to masses of people, no one can even communicate everything he knows about himself to a few contemporaries. It is easier to publicize one's name, as opposed to details about one's life, but merely having someone know one's name means nothing. Bill would be no different if his name were Bob. One's name says nothing about the namebearer. This is clear from the fact that people can successfully assume false names or legally change their names. Indeed, names are conferred before any characteristics of the namebearer are evident. Moreover, even with respect to well-known people (e.g., Charles Richter, for whom the earthquake magnitude scale is named), observers who merely recognize the name still know nothing about the person to whom the name refers— that complex intersection of characteristics that make up the person.

And what substantive information one is able to communicate about himself to even his most intimate associates is subject to erroneous propagation and interpretation. In any event, it is soon forgotten or pushed out of their consciousnesses. Moreover, those who do accurately remember fail to make a complete transfer of what they do remember to their survivors. So, the memory of those who have died diminishes over time. In fact, most of the some 106 billion persons who have lived upon the earth[8] are now forgotten by those of us still living. In other words, no other human being ever presently thinks about them at all.

Further, our human memories are easily confused, and we quickly forget. Even for the famous—after the moment of silence or day of mourning concludes—the flags go back to full staff, the sound of the 21-gun salute fades, tears are dried, and he is soon forgotten. As the Preacher in Ecclesiastes says, "There is no lasting remembrance of the wise man as with the fool, inasmuch as in the coming days all will be forgotten. And how the wise man and the fool alike die!" (Ecclesiastes 2:16).

Even the authors of great ideas are all but forgotten. We do not remember Edison every time a light switch is thrown, nor do we remember Alexander Graham Bell every time someone answers the phone or opens an invoice from a telecommunications company named Bell.

American poet Fitz-Greene Halleck (1790–1867) illustrates the fleeting nature of fame. Edgar Allan Poe once wrote that "no name in the American poetical world is more firmly established" than

Halleck's.[9] A statue of Halleck stands in the Literary Walk of New York's Central Park. Yet today Halleck is all but forgotten.[10]

The distinction between the famous and the non-famous appears to us to be great and in effect the difference in leaving a mark, or being significant, and not. We all observe the familiar hierarchy of fame, on which people are graded by the mark they appear to have left on the world. If it were diagrammed, the highest and lowest levels would look something like this:

Those who reach the pinnacle of fame (e.g., George Washington) and are widely known over many generations

Those who are "unknown" or forgotten by every other person within a few weeks of death

But this apparent wide disparity is in reality an illusion. In terms of the totality of time and space, no human stands truly significant based merely on the extent to which he is known by other humans. As Dante says in his *Divine Comedy*, the "noise of worldly fame is but a blast of wind, that blows from diverse points, and shifts its name," so that one who lives to an old age has no advantage over one who dies as a baby.[11]

As discussed earlier, eponymy, or the practice of naming something for a person, is common in many human societies. Although it might appear that having something named for one provides a surefire path to leaving a legacy, this too, upon inspection, fades into a mirage. An initial problem is that things are frequently not appropriately named. University of Chicago professor Stephen Stigler argues that "no scientific discovery is ever named after its original discoverer." Ironically, this contention has become known as Stigler's Law, making Stigler's name itself an eponym.[12]

Moreover, even if appropriately named, the connection to the person for whom the thing is named inevitably fades away. The building is torn down or renamed, the bridge replaced, the organization disbanded, and the concept supplanted. Even where the eponymous name continues to be used, people often no longer recognize it as related to the person for whom the thing is named.

There are many examples of faded eponymy. The state of Maryland is named in honor of Queen Henrietta Maria of England, wife of King Charles I. Tasmania is named for A. J. Tasman, a Dutch navigator. The diesel engine is named for Rudolph Diesel. The Fahrenheit temperature scale is named for Gabriel Daniel Fahrenheit. Braille is named for Louis Braille, a Frenchman. The poinsettia plant is named for Joel Roberts Poinsett, the first US Minister to Mexico.

The graham cracker and graham flour are named for Sylvester Graham, an American minister who sought in the 1830s to introduce a whole-grain alternative to unhealthy food. The medical test we call the Pap smear is named for George Papanicolaou, M.D., a doctor who was born in Greece and later worked at Cornell Medical School in New York City. The saxophone is named for Adolphe Sax, a Belgian who made musical instruments. The electrical unit of the volt is named for Count Alessandron Volta, an Italian physicist. And the Jacuzzi bath is named for Candido Jacuzzi, an engineer in California who developed the device in order to help his disabled son.

It is safe to say, however, that few people today recognize these eponymous names or many others as signifying the persons from whom the names derive. In other words, we use these eponymous words constantly but never think, and usually are unaware, of the person for whom the thing is named. As one writer says, "Most eponyms die. Few outlive the fame of the people who birthed them, and most fade even faster."[13]

Not only are there persons for whom things are named who are no longer recognized as the source of the eponymous word, but also there are eponymous words that almost no one recognizes as derived from the name of a person. For instance, there is a bridge on the outskirts of New York City called Outerbridge Crossing. Most persons undoubtedly suppose, if they think of the meaning of the name at all, that it refers to the bridge's location at the edge of the city. Instead, the bridge is named in honor of the now forgotten Eugenius Harvey Outerbridge.[14]

It is not just that the connections are often lost between eponymously named places and things and the persons who supply those names. In addition, the eponymous name is sometimes attributed to the wrong person. These could be called broken significations or misdirected eponymy. For example, many people think that Grant Park in Atlanta is named for Ulysses S. Grant, which would be unlikely, because Grant, along with William T. Sherman, was responsible for the conquest and burning of Atlanta in 1864 during the Civil War. Instead, the park is named for Lemuel P. Grant, a Confederate officer who fought against the Union forces and donated the land for the park to the city.[15] But very few Atlantans know of Lemuel Grant.

A newspaper journalist has observed, "After it seemed that almost every bridge, highway, section of highway, rest stop, rotary, underpass and overpass in Connecticut had been named for someone no one ever heard of, the Legislature rested."[16] Dolores Hayden, a Yale University professor, calls the signs naming places for politicians "litter on a stick."[17] She says name signs are uninformative, a waste of money, and a distraction. She explains that the signs don't tell anything about the person being honored.[18]

The impossibility of attaining a satisfactory significance in the minds of other people is clear from this thought. If all people who had ever lived knew every thought, word, and action of mine and lived in constant reference to me, I would still be utterly insignificant in any total sense, because humanity even in the aggregate is nothing in this vast universe and in the eternity of time. As Boethius says, "But ye, when ye think on future fame, fancy it an immortality that you are begetting for yourselves. Why, if thou scannest the infinite spaces of eternity, what room hast thou left for rejoicing in the durability of thy name?" He adds, "So it comes to pass that fame, though it extend to ever so wide a space of years, if it be compared to never-lessening eternity, seems not short-lived merely, but altogether nothing."[19]

Not only do people forget, but monuments and buildings disappear or lose their commemorative function. The weather soon washes the name from the tombstone. An archaeologist, returning from an expedition in the Near East, echoes Ecclesiastes with these words:

> We dug and dug until, at a depth of sixty feet, we uncovered the remains of a civilization 6000 years old. It had begun somehow flourished for a while, and then had withered and died. It lay buried in its own dust. Immediately on top of that burial ground were the relics of another civilization, and so on. As I climbed out of that pit sixty feet deep, with each of my sixty steps I traversed one century of blood, sweat, and tears. There— layer upon layer—was a cross section of human history, 6,000 years of it. And when, at the end of the day, I reached the top, look as I might in every direction, I could see nothing but vast, empty, barren desert waste. And I said, "Vanity of Vanities. All is vanity."[20]

Percy Bysshe Shelley's "Ozymandias" also dramatizes the inconsequentiality of the grandest human efforts at significance:

> I met a traveler from an antique land
> Who said: "Two vast and trunkless legs of stone
> Stand in the desert. Near them, on the sand,
> Half sunk, a shattered visage lies, whose frown,
> And wrinkled lip, and sneer of cold command,
> Tell that its sculptor well those passions read
> Which yet survive, stamped on these lifeless things,
> The hand that mocked them and the heart that fed:
> And on the pedestal these words appear:
> 'My name is Ozymandias, king of kings:
> Look on my works, ye Mighty, and despair!'
> Nothing beside remains. Round the decay
> Of that colossal wreck, boundless and bare
> The lone and level sands stretch far away."[21]

Besides the passage of time, earthquakes, floods, hurricanes, and tornadoes remind us that even the most permanent of man's creations are temporary.

Centuries ago inscribed funerary urns were buried in shallow soils in Norfolk, England. Their excavation inspired Sir Thomas Browne to write an essay called "Urn Burial," in which he notes the impossibility of discovering "who were the proprietaries of these bones" and how the owners of them had "so grossly erred in the art of perpetuation." Recognizing the difficulty of reading "bare inscriptions" on ancient graves, Browne exposes the futile human penchant "to hope for eternity by enigmatical epithets or first letters of our names."[22] In other words, today we have no idea who these people are and the inscriptions on the urns stand useless in identifying them or perpetuating their memories.

In fact, today, before our eyes, ancient monuments are deteriorating. In some areas historic relics and ruins are so numerous that they are practically impossible to preserve.[23] As Albert Camus says, "nothing of the conqueror lasts, not even his doctrines."[24]

In short, man is too finite to have more than a superficial understanding of what happened in the past. For example, what philosophy prevailed in 1815 in England or what caused the Peloponnesian Wars? At least 99.9 percent of all that happens sneaks by unrecorded. We don't even know the identity of the unknown soldier buried at Arlington National Cemetery near Washington, D.C. And, furthermore, even what we do manage to preserve is soon destroyed or forgotten. Consider, for instance, the myriad of exhibits in historical museums. No one could possibly see all these things, which are but a fraction of the past, and even what can be seen slips out of our memories like water through a sieve.

So we all remain, despite our frantic efforts, apparently utterly insignificant. Again, Camus movingly describes the dreadful feeling of insignificance that overwhelms a dying man:

> What is more exceptional in our town is the difficulty
> one may experience in dying . . . . Think of what it must
> be for a dying man, trapped behind hundreds of walls

all sizzling with heat, while the whole population,
sitting in cafes on the telephone, is discussing
shipments, bills of lading, discounts![25]

Much depression probably results from the feeling of insignificance or unimportance. The more one sees his life slipping silently by, the more frantic becomes his grasping for attention. When one fails at something—doesn't make the team, loses the campaign—it often seems to be a tragedy. But even when one does win or come out on top it provides little pleasure. The feeling of satisfaction is short-lived.

What one could have done but did not do, the road not taken, looms as irretrievably and tragically lost. The melancholy of Thomas Gray's "Elegy Written in a Country Churchyard," a plaintive speculation on what the poor might have been had they received opportunity, results:

Perhaps in this neglected spot is laid
Some heart once pregnant with celestial fire;
Hands that the rod of empire might have swayed
Or waked to ecstacy the living lyre.

But Knowledge to their eyes her ample page
Rich with the spoils of time did ne'er unroll;
Chill Penury repress'd their noble rage,
And froze the genial current of the soul.

Full many a gem of purest ray serene,
The dark unfathom'd caves of ocean bear:
Full many a flower is born to blush unseen,
And waste its sweetness on the desert air.

Some village Hampden that with dauntless breast
The little tyrant of his fields withstood;
Some mute inglorious Milton here may rest,
Some Cromwell guiltless of his country's blood.[26]

It seems that each of us remains utterly insignificant against the expanse of space and time. But are we content to accept oblivion as our fate?

Questions for Reflection

1. What is your reaction to the words of Psalm 103:14-16 that our "days are like grass" or a flower that blooms in the morning and dies in the afternoon, and one whose "place acknowledges it no longer"?

2. What do you think of the story of Haman, who bragged about his position, possessions, and family when he thought that Mordecai failed to acknowledge his importance? Did these accomplishments seem to satisfy Haman?

3. Is it possible for a single person to be significant across the vast expanse of space and time? In other words, do the efforts of even the most famous among us, as George Washington, ramify through enough of space and time to make them known and remembered throughout reality?

4. Can a person record enough of his thoughts and activities or save enough of her memorabilia and artifacts, to make him or her significant? Why or why not?

5. Does human history form a complete and accurate record of human thought and activity? Can human beings even create such a history? Why do you think so?

6. Is it feasible to preserve all human artifacts that are considered historically significant? If so, what could be done with all of them? Are the museums of the world sufficient to accommodate them and could anyone even see and remember most of them?

7. Would having something (such as a bridge, building, invention, or mountain) named for you make you significant? Why or why not?

8. What are examples of things that are named for persons and later the connection between the name and the person was forgotten? What does this say about the ability of eponymy (or naming things for people) to secure individual significance?

6. The Persistent Yearning for Significance

Of all things in the world, people are the most precious.
    —Declaration of the United Nations Conference
    on the Human Environment

The ultimate goal should be the fulfillment of the potential for growth in each human personality—not for the favored few, but for all of humankind. . . . Humanism can provide the purpose and inspiration that so many seek; it can give personal meaning and significance to human life.
    —Humanist Manifesto II[1]

If there is no God and people are mere random collections of particles, then, objectively speaking, they have no greater value than any other random collections of particles—such as animals, plants, rocks, mud, or cosmic gas. Bertrand Russell is correct when he says that science (without God) presents a world that stands "purposeless" and "void of meaning." Russell explains:

> That man is the product of causes which had no prevision of the end they were achieving; that his origin, his growth, his hopes and his beliefs, are but the outcome of accidental collocations of atoms; that no fire, no heroism, no intensity of thought and feeling can preserve an individual life beyond the grave; that all the labours of all the ages, all the devotion, all the inspiration, all the noonday brightness of human genius are destined to extinction in the vast death of the solar

> system, and that the whole temple of man's achievement must inevitably be buried beneath the debris of a universe in ruins—all these things, if not quite beyond dispute, are yet so nearly certain that no philosophy which rejects them can hope to stand. Only within the scaffolding of these truths, only on the firm foundation of unyielding despair, can the soul's habitation henceforth be safely built.[2]

Perhaps unintentionally illustrating this view, the modern animal rights movement insists that "all animals are equal" and that to consider humans as more important than non-human animals is to practice "specieism," a new offense to political correctness.[3]

Under this approach, we find ourselves trapped by the conclusion that all life (human and non-human) is absurd and equally so. As John-Paul Sartre says, it is indeed "absurd that we are born."[4]

But we do not seem to be content with this gloomy outlook. Despite the hard objectivity of our insignificance as individuals on a materialistic view, we defiantly insist that we stand significant, that somehow we are important. Most of us assert, without apparent foundation, that we as individuals command more importance than any animals or other non-human things. The United Nations Conference on the Human Environment, which met in Stockholm in 1972, states, "Of all things in the world, people are the most precious."[5] The *Humanist Manifesto II* was written one year later. The value it places on human life does not derive, it says, from any theology. Its signers are "non-theists" who "begin with humans not God." It echoes the UN statement: "The preciousness and dignity of the individual person is a central humanist value."[6] But material reality by itself gives us no basis for these sentiments.

In addition to these unsupported but glowing affirmations of the preeminent value of human life, we find other incongruous facts. For instance, despite the apparent complete insignificance of the human individual, even the most obscure person on this planet takes some interest in his appearance and is subject to embarrassment. Too, all persons bristle with indignation when affronted, and other persons condone that indignation—reactions that do not seem appropriate if individual humans are as insignificant as they appear to be on a materialistic account of reality.[7]

We also inexplicably shrink from the brevity of life that appears to be our fate. British Enlightenment thinker John Stuart Mill says in *On Religion* that "not annihilation but immortality may be the burdensome idea."[8] But most people do not act as if that is the case. As writer Judith Sargent Murray recognizes, the desire of a human being to survive in the "bosom of posterity seems interwoven with our existence."[9] Woody Allen says it this way: "I don't want to achieve immortality through my work. I want to achieve it through not dying." Indeed, as Spanish philosopher-poet Miguel de Unamuno puts it, "We cannot conceive ourselves as not existing."[10] Every time you try to think of it, you see yourself as an observer watching and surviving your demise.

The promise by eastern religions of the merger of the individual human into the monistic whole provides no more comfort than does materialism. Again, Unamuno speaks for most when he says, "Tricks of monism avail us nothing; we crave the substance and not the shadow of immortality."[11]

In fact, we recoil from death and imagine and act as if our earthly lives here will go on indefinitely or even forever. This can be seen as a way of insisting on our significance. As Paul Bowles observes, because we don't know the date of our coming deaths we imagine that our earthly lives are "limitless":

> Death is always on the way, but the fact that you don't know when it will arrive seems to take away from the finiteness of life. It's that terrible precision that we hate so much. But because we don't know, we get to think of life as an inexhaustible well. Yet everything only happens a certain number of times, really. . . . How many more times will you watch the full moon rise? Perhaps twenty. And yet it all seems limitless.[12]

The young especially are prone to see their lives as unending—that is, they mistake the absence of known temporal boundaries for no boundaries at all. One novelist has written about "those early amorphous years when memory has only begun, when life is full of beginnings and no ends and everything was forever."[13]

Many songs and poems capture our sentiments about longevity. We sing: "The Rockies may tumble, Gibraltar may crumble, They're only made of clay. But . . . our love is here to stay"; "I will always love you"; "I will never leave you"; and "far beyond forever you'll be mine."

But the evidence we see does not remotely support these sentiments. People are always leaving, becoming seriously ill, and dying. We and our relationships are, in biblical terms, much more like the extreme transience of a vapor (James 4:14), breath (Psalm 39:5, 11), or flower that blooms for one day and then dies (Psalm 103:15-16; Psalm 90:5-6; 1 Peter 1:24).

Consider the concept of life expectancy. The current life expectancy in the United States is 77.7 years at birth.[14] As one gets older, his life expectancy increases; that is, the horizon resets. At least until we get to 75 years or so, we all comfort ourselves with the thought that we have at least x (the difference in our current age and our life expectancy) more years. But a large percentage of people do not live to their life expectancy. Some die at 6 months, 1 year, 10, 21, 35 years, and so forth. Yet we blithely assume that we all have at least until our published life expectancies (or secretly we believe that we will outlive them because we exercise, eat lots of broccoli, and someone in our families lived to be 96 years of age).

We also insist on our individual significance in other ways. Legal systems recognize claims for misconduct that demeans the dignity of the individual. These include slander, libel, outrage, false imprisonment, false arrest, malicious prosecution, mistreatment of the body of a deceased person, and others. Moreover, surviving family members can recover for a decedent's pain.[15] Awards to survivors obviously do not compensate the deceased. Nor are they intended to

85

compensate the deceased's family for its monetary loss. Often, the family has suffered no monetary loss, particularly in the death of a child.[16] The primary purpose served by awards like this is apparently to affirm the significance of the deceased as a human being, just as do awards for the mistreatment of a corpse. But, as we have seen, these legal doctrines and awards assume a great deal of individual significance that is not apparent.

We, despite the contrary evidence, feel that our thoughts, words, and actions are significant. Even though I am apparently replaceable and inconsequential, I feel that I am unique. And the very existence of this desire for significance implies the existence of its fulfillment, just as hunger implies the existence of food. As Francis Schaeffer says, if man is not significant he is the lowest of all creatures: "The green moss on the rock is higher than he, for it can be fulfilled in the universe which exists . . . man (not only individually but as a race), being unfulfillable, is dead. In this situation men should not walk on the grass, but respect it—for it is higher than he!"[17]

The common and thoughtlessly used expression "God only knows" articulates man's desperate hope that somebody is watching. But is anyone there?

Questions for Reflection

1. If people are merely accidental collections of particles, do they have any greater value than any other objects in the world—such as plants, rocks, and non-human animals? How would you support your view?

2. Secular humanism says that individual humans have supreme importance, and these sentiments seem noble. But does a materialistic view of reality (such as secular humanism) provide any logical basis for its view of the high value of human life? Why or why not?

3. What do you think about animal liberation views that humans are no more important than non-human organisms? If you disagree with that view, how would you reason against it?

4. Are you content to accept the meaninglessness and obscurity of individual human lives that is dictated by a materialist view of reality? Why or why not?

5. Despite the apparent insignificance of human individuals, how do we try to insist on our significance?

6. What do these efforts to insist on individual significance say about the needs of people?

7. In what ways do we seek to enlarge our individual significance?

Section II:
The True Significance of the Individual Person

7. Made in the Image of God

God created man in His own image, in the image of God He created him; male and female He created them.
                                             —Genesis 1:27

"Look at the birds of the air, that they do not sow, nor reap, nor gather into barns, and yet your heavenly Father feeds them. Are you not worth much more than they?"
                                             —Matthew 7:26

How does Christianity, if it is true, change the gloomy picture of insignificance? Do the tenets of Christianity address the yearning for individual significance?

The compelling message is that Christianity describes the incredible, in fact total, significance of every individual person. It transforms the picture of insignificance as the morning sun transforms the predawn. Four doctrines or teachings of Christianity pertain directly to our individual significance as human beings. But few of us appreciate the value these teachings have for our individual significance. These teachings form the equivalent of an uncashed check of inestimable value in one's wallet.

Perhaps the most important biblical teaching on the individual's significance is that each person is created in the image of God, or *imago dei*. According to Genesis 1:26-27,

91

> Then God said, "Let Us make man in Our image, according to Our likeness; and let them rule over the fish of the sea and over the birds of the sky and over the cattle and over all the earth, and over every creeping thing that creeps on the earth." God created man in His own image, in the image of God He created him; male and female He created them.

The Christian view of individual human significance stands in stark contrast to most non-Christian views. We have seen what Bertrand Russell and scientific materialism say about the importance of the human individual. Under that view, all objects in the universe are random collections of particles and have no intrinsic value. A human being is no different.

Those who are intellectually honest must recognize that materialism leads to the rejection of all moral values and the significance of the human individual. Assume for the moment that centers of conscious and reliable thought could result from the random shuffling of particles, which, from our empirical knowledge, is impossible.[1] But even if reflective consciousness and veridical perception and thought could be produced by blind forces, how could such random processes produce any valid and binding moral standards for behavior? They obviously could not. No arbitrary arrangement of particles could be said to have any more intrinsic value than any other. Under this scenario, killing someone and eating him is no less virtuous than shaking his hand. Both events are merely random sequences of particle behavior.

Russell tells us that we can "safely" build our lives on this "firm foundation of unyielding despair."[2] But how could "unyielding despair" provide a "firm foundation" for one's life or anything else? Rather, it seems that materialism leads to the conclusion that life and what appears to be real are irredeemably absurd and utterly meaningless.

One writer who with unflinching honesty recognizes this consequence for the value of individual human life is Friedrich Nietzsche. Embracing nihilism, or the denial of all moral values, he says, "There are no moral phenomena at all, but only a moral interpretation of phenomena."[3] Singing the praises of the will to power, which he considers the essential life force,[4] Nietzsche insists: "I do not point to the evil and pain of existence with the finger of reproach, but rather entertain the hope that life may one day be more evil and more full of suffering than it has ever been."[5] Thus, he can pronounce: "The great majority of men have no right to life."[6]

Adam Gottlieb follows the same nihilistic trail but in the direction of self-destructive hedonism. In *The Pleasures of Cocaine*, he argues that Western society has arrived at a "Golden Age of Decadence," in which cocaine and other recreational drugs should be freely enjoyed. According to Gottlieb, "illusory moral values are in a state of rapid collapse," and decadence "is an inevitable part of history and progress."[7] He argues that "if there is any teleological purpose to man's existence on earth and in his power to progress, it is that he should achieve a successful form of decadence and learn to live in harmony with it. The life-game then would be, at least in part, to sustain a decadent situation for as long as one might expect any civilization to last and perhaps longer."[8]

Aleister Crowley could serve as a poster child for the end result of moral nihilism. His message is, "Do what thou wilt shall be the whole of the Law."[9] This has become a mantra for many in Western society, especially rock-and-roll artists.[10] Accordingly, Crowley lived as a drug addict, occultist, sexual libertine, sadomasochist, and reputed pedophile.[11]

Eastern religions also give no value to the human individual. According to Buddhism, the distinctions that we think we see among individual persons constitute illusions. In fact, "all appearances are viewed as illusions," and "the self is a fiction." Buddhist "meditation on the reasonings of no-self" aspires to reach "the understanding that no self or essence exists."[12] In Hindu mysticism, the world of differentiation is also illusion (maya), and salvation consists of realizing that God (Brahman), who is infinite and includes all attributes and properties, and self (Atman) are identical.[13] Moreover, these Eastern religions offer the individual person the ultimate goal of breaking the cycle of reincarnation and merging back into the monistic pool of existence (nirvana in Buddhism and moksa in Hinduism).[14]

Marxism and socialism also place little value on the individual. Rather, the state or society serves as the most important reality.[15]

Consistent with this outlook, North Korean communist officials have told prisoners when entering confinement there: "You are not a human being anymore."[16]

Another increasingly prevalent non-Christian view regarding the value of individual human life comes from the animal rights movement. You may have heard the light-hearted slogan "Pets are people too," which is sometimes used in ads for animal hospitals and pet stores. However, Ingrid Newkirk, head of People for the Ethical Treatment of Animals (PETA), believes just that. According to her, "A rat is a pig is a dog is a boy. They are all mammals."[17] In other words, human beings are not superior in value to other organisms.

In contrast to these non-monotheistic views, the doctrine of the *imago dei*, that individual people are made in God's image, sets every individual human above everything that is not human. Nothing else in creation, even other forms of life, bears God's image. Jesus comforted his disciples with these words: "Do not fear; you are more valuable than many sparrows" (Matthew 10:31; Luke 12:6-7). On another occasion Jesus justified healing on the Sabbath by asking rhetorically, "How much more valuable then is a man than a sheep!" (Matthew 12:11-12).

Many other biblical teachings also place greater value on human life than on nonhuman life and immaterial objects. God gives humankind dominion over the rest of nature (Genesis 1:26-31; Psalm 8:6-8). God instituted the sacrifice of animals because of human sin (Genesis 3:21). Nonhuman life is also punished for human sin in many accounts, including the flood (Genesis 6:5-7; 7:21-23), a destruction of trees (2 Kings 3:19; Isaiah 10:33-34), and Jesus' casting the legion of demons from the Gerasene man into a herd of swine, which then rushed off a cliff into the sea (Mark 5:1-17).

As stated, the individual human's distinction as the image bearer of God makes him not only more important than other life forms but also of greater significance than anything else in nature. In other words, a single person carries more value than the entire nonhuman universe. In the words of Miguel de Unamuno, "A human soul is worth all the universe."[18] In fact, God cursed the entire world because of the sin of one man (Genesis 3:17-18). And all creation, we are told, "groans and suffers" in this affliction while anxiously awaiting God's final judgment (Romans 8:19-22; 1 Chronicles 16:31-35).

But the image of God does not give individual people significance between each other. All people bear the same image of God. If I, as an individual, did not exist, there would be nothing less than there now is, given just this doctrine. However, there is much more to the significance of the individual human than his status as a bearer of God's image.

Questions for Reflection

1. What does the Christian doctrine that people are made in God's image mean? Is anything else in the created universe made in God's image?

2. What value does being created in God's image confer on individual human beings?

3. What do other religions say about the value of individual persons?

4. According to scientific materialism, a human being is a random collection of particles that was accidentally formed by blind chance and has no purpose or destiny other than extinction. On this view, what value does the individual person have?

5. What enduring or meaningful basis do non-Christian views of reality (including atheistic scientific materialism, Marxism, and other religions) offer for morality? Can you think of any persons whose thinking illustrates these views?

6. Does the fact that a person is made in God's image by itself furnish her with an adequate or complete significance? Why or why not?

8. Known by the Omnipresent, Eternal, and Omniscient God

"But the very hairs of your head are all numbered. So do not fear."

—Matthew 10:30-31

Here rests in honored glory an American soldier known but to God.
—Inscription on Tomb of the Unknowns, Arlington National Cemetery, Arlington, Virginia

He knows my name
He knows my every thought
He sees each tear that falls
And He hears me when I call
—Tommy Walker, "He Knows My Name" (1996)

A second set of Christian doctrines also speaks to the question of our individual significance, namely, the transcendent attributes of God. Christian Scripture teaches that God is omnipresent, eternal, and omniscient. These characteristics of God are a powerful multiplier of individual human significance.

God is omnipresent: He inhabits all of space. He exists on Jupiter as much as he does on earth. David gives us the clearest biblical description of God's omnipresence in Psalm 139:7-10:

Where can I go from Your Spirit?
Or where can I flee from Your presence?

> If I ascend to heaven, You are there;
> If I make my bed in Sheol, behold, You are there.
> If I take the wings of the dawn,
> If I dwell in the remotest part of the sea,
> Even there Your hand will lead me,
> And Your right hand will lay hold of me.

Later, Solomon explains that although he is building a temple for God, "the heavens and the highest heavens cannot contain Him" (2 Chronicles 2:5-6).

God is also eternal: No time has passed or will pass without him. God told Moses, "I live forever" (Deuteronomy 32:40). The psalmist says, "Blessed be the LORD, the God of Israel, from everlasting even to everlasting" (Psalm 106:48). God had no beginning: "Your throne is established from of old; You are from everlasting" (Psalm 93:2). And he has no end:

> "Of old You founded the earth,
> and the heavens are the work of Your hands.
> "Even they will perish, but You endure;
> And all of them will wear out like a garment;
> Like clothing You will change them and they
> will be changed.
> "But You are the same,
> And Your years will not come to an end."
> (Psalm 102:25-27)

God always is. In fact, one of the names of God in the Bible is "I AM" (Exodus 3:11-14).

Not only does God exist everywhere in space and time, but also he knows everything that it is possible to know. In other words, he is omniscient, or all-knowing. No occurrence has ever slipped by God; he never gets tired and nods off. According to Psalm 121:3-4,

> He will not allow your foot to slip;
> He who keeps you will not slumber.
> Behold, He who keeps Israel
> Will neither slumber nor sleep.

God is presently and completely aware of everything that has ever happened and is now happening in every corner of space. Most Christians also believe that God is presently aware of everything that will happen in the future. The psalmist says, "He counts the number of the stars; He gives names to all of them" (Psalm 147:4). Solomon adds, "Sheol and Abaddon lie open before the LORD" (Proverbs 15:11). The earth too with its incomprehensible, nonstop profusion of human activity is exhaustively known by God: "For He looks to the ends of the earth and sees everything under the heavens" (Job 28:24). Human beings, even collectively, could not begin to know and distinguish each individual bird that has lived, but God never forgets a single sparrow (Luke 12:6-7). And it's not just sparrows that attract God's attention. God says,

> "For every beast of the forest is Mine,
> The cattle on a thousand hills.

"I know every bird of the mountains,
And everything that moves in the field is Mine."
(Psalm 50:10-11)

Most relevant to us, however, this omnipresent and eternal God knows exhaustively every detail about each person who has ever lived. Paul takes comfort in being "fully known" by God (1 Corinthians 13:12)[1] and says that one day he will understand the full implications of this truth—even though "now we see through a glass, darkly" (1 Corinthians 13:12 KJV).

Psalm 87:6 says, "The LORD will count when He registers the peoples, 'This one was born there [Zion].' " But God doesn't just count us. We are also told:

Many, O LORD my God, are the wonders
        which You have done,
And Your thoughts toward us;
There is none to compare with You.
If I would declare and speak of them,
They would be too numerous to count. (Psalm 40:5)

In Psalm 139:1-4, 17-18, David describes God's complete awareness of individual persons:

O LORD, You have searched me and known me.
You know when I sit down and when I rise up;
You understand my thought from afar.
You scrutinize my path and my lying down,
and are intimately acquainted with all my ways.

Even before there is a word on my tongue,
Behold, O LORD, You know it all. . . .

How precious also are Your thoughts to me, O God!
How vast is the sum of them!
If I should count them, they would outnumber the sand.
When I awake, I am still with You.

Old Testament scholar Bruce Waltke summarizes Psalm 139:

> In the first paragraph, David celebrates the fact that
> God knows all about him, all the time, and in every
> place. In the second paragraph he sings that God is
> always present with him, whether in heaven or in the
> grave. In the third paragraph he proves these truths.
> God, You created me, You know me inside out, and
> look where you [sic] made your magnum opus—in the
> dark watery chamber of my mother's womb. You might
> just as well have made me in the bowels of the earth. In
> the last paragraph David tells us he is celebrating God's
> omnipotence and omnipresence in the presence of
> murderers who hate him and want to kill him.[2]

As God told the nation of Assyria, "I know your sitting down, and
your going out and your coming in, and your raging against Me" (2
Kings 19:27). God even numbers our steps (Job 31:4) and counts the
hairs on our heads (Matthew 10:30). This describes an immense
significance. Every time an individual pulls a hair out of his head,
there is impact in all of space and the remainder of eternity as the
eternal God updates his count.

All the thoughts and intents of individual humans are open before God. As David told his son Solomon: "The LORD searches all hearts, and understands every intent of the thoughts" (1 Chronicles 28:9).[3] In another passage, David was talking to God and abruptly stopped with these words: "Again what more can David say to You? For You know Your servant, O LORD God!" (2 Samuel 7:20). In other words, David acknowledged that he cannot tell God anything about himself that God does not already know. In the Sermon on the Mount, Jesus says the intentions of people will be punished as well as their acts, which means that God knows our thoughts (Matthew 5:21-22, 27-28). Too, Jesus condemned the scribes and Pharisees who outwardly appeared righteous but inwardly were grossly diseased with sin (Matthew 23:25-28).[4]

God's omniscience extends to our difficulties and struggles. David says, "I will rejoice and be glad in Your lovingkindness, because You have seen my affliction; You have known the troubles of my soul" (Psalm 31:7). David expands: "You have taken account of my wanderings; put my tears in Your bottle. Are they not in Your book?" (Psalm 56:8). God also knows our weaknesses and limitations: "For He Himself knows our frame; He is mindful that we are but dust" (Psalm 103:14).

God's awareness includes our sinful actions, thoughts, and intentions. Evil is significant. God does not turn his back and refuse to look. Proverbs affirms, "The eyes of the LORD are in every place, watching the evil and the good" (Proverbs 15:3).[5] For example, Jesus knew, without being told, that the Samaritan woman at the well in Sychar had been married to five husbands and was then living with a man who was not her husband (John 4:16-19). Ezra laments that the sin of Israel "has grown even to the heavens" (Ezra 9:6). Thus, even the person who refuses to accept Christ and otherwise obey God does not suffer the ultimate indignity of losing his significance.

With God, no act is secret. One cannot escape God's notice by acting at night or whispering in a soundproof room. And a crime cannot be concealed by killing all the witnesses, wearing gloves that don't leave fingerprints, or shredding incriminating documents. Jesus warned, "There is nothing covered up that will not be revealed, and hidden that will not be known. Accordingly whatever you have said in the dark will be heard in the light, and what you have whispered in the inner rooms will be proclaimed upon the housetops" (Luke 12:1-3).[6] As David says,

> Where can I go from Your Spirit?
> Or where can I flee from Your presence? . . .
>
> If I say, "Surely the darkness will overwhelm me,
> and the light around me will be night,"
> Even the darkness is not dark to You,
> And the night is as bright as the day.
> Darkness and light are alike to You. (Psalm 139:7, 11-12)

Because God knows that which we try to conceal, he is able to judge our secrets: "God will bring every act to judgment, everything which is hidden, whether it is good or evil" (Ecclesiastes 12:14). Paul writes that "God will judge the secrets of men through Jesus Christ" (Romans 2:16).

In fact, God knows us better than we know ourselves. We don't know the number of hairs on our heads, as he does (Matthew 10:30-31). God knows every minute detail of our lives—things that our finite minds cannot contain. God, for example, knows how many times I sneezed last year. When Peter vigorously, and no doubt sincerely, vowed that he would never deny his Lord, Jesus knew that Peter would deny him after the betrayal (Matthew 26:31-35, 69-75). Jesus also knew that the same Pharisees who said, "If we had been living in the days of our fathers, we would not have been partners with them in shedding the blood of the prophets," would persecute and kill prophets who would come later (Matthew 23:29-30).

And God will not forget us. According to Hebrews 6:10, "God is not unjust so as to forget your work and the love which you have shown toward His name, in having ministered and in still ministering to the saints."

Alongside God's omniscience, human self-kept history is extremely sketchy and inaccurate. We attempt in our human history to record and explain what only God knows. The completeness of God's knowledge of man's activities and thoughts underlies Jesus' condemnation of the cities in which he had done most of his miracles but which had failed to repent. Jesus castigated the cities of Chorazin, Bethsaida, and Capernaum, saying that if these same miracles had been done in Tyre, Sidon, and Sodom, which were considered the nadir of evil, they would have repented (Matthew 11:20-24). God apparently was so aware of the minds of these long-dead people that he could say what would have persuaded them to repent.

What God knows, he never forgets. "The eyes of the LORD preserve knowledge," Proverbs 22:12 says. The Psalms also attest to the faithfulness of God's memory: "Your name, O LORD, is everlasting, Your remembrance, O LORD, throughout all generations" (Psalm 135:13). Forgiven sin is the only thing that God forgets, and that by his choice. David describes God's forgiveness: "As far as the east is from the west, so far has He removed our transgressions from us" (Psalm 103:12).

Because God knows everything perfectly (i.e., as well as it could be known), nothing receives any more attention than anything else. And God is always aware of, or attends to, all that he knows. In other words, it is in his immediate cognizance. Theologian Charles Hodge says that "all things are ever present in his view."[7] A well-known writer from outside the realm of theology also comments on God's awareness of individual humans: "The Deity does not regard the human race collectively. He surveys at one glance and severally all the beings of whom mankind is composed, and he discerns in each man the resemblances which assimilate him to all his fellows, and differences which distinguish him from them."[8]

Thus, a trite thought of a person stands equally known to God as another person's revolutionary idea. In this sense, a fumble is just as significant as a touchdown, an F no less significant than an A. Nor does size affect the attention that God gives something. He is equally cognizant of an amoeba and the Empire State Building.

And no person commands any more importance than any other person before God. He knows all things equally and is not a respecter of persons. The bald man is not less significant because he has fewer hairs for God to number. "For there is no partiality with God," Paul says in Romans 2:11. Moses agrees: "For the LORD your God is the God of gods and the Lord of lords, the great, the mighty, and the awesome God who does not show partiality" (Deuteronomy 10:17). Jesus invites all persons to come to him: "Come to Me, all who are weary and heavy-laden, and I will give you rest" (Matthew 11:28). "The Lord . . . is not wishing for any to perish but for all to come to repentance" (2 Peter 3:9).

With God, the Gentile stands equal in importance to the Jew (Romans 10:12; 1 Corinthians 12:13; Galatians 3:28; Colossians 3:11). Recall that John the Baptist told the Jewish multitudes that being descendants of Abraham carried no importance with God: "Do not begin to say to yourselves, 'We have Abraham for our father,' for I say to you that from these stones God is able to raise up children to Abraham" (Luke 3:7-8).

In Genesis, the Egyptian maid Hagar participated with Abraham and Sarah in their spectacular effort to hurry God's promise of a child. Abraham and Hagar had relations that produced Ishmael, who became the father of the Arab people.[9] Nevertheless, when Hagar fled for her life, God saw and gave "heed" to her affliction (Genesis 16:11-13).

Indicating God's equal regard for all persons, Jesus asked a Samaritan woman, to whom most Jews would not have spoken, for a drink (John 4:9-10). And the Holy Spirit instructed Peter to take the gospel to the house of Cornelius, a Gentile who feared God. This was the initial spread of the gospel to non-Jewish persons. After Peter received this instruction to preach Christ to those formerly considered unclean, he said, "I most certainly understand that God is not one to show partiality, but in every nation the man who fears Him and does what is right is welcome to Him" (Acts 10:34-35).

God considers even very sinful people as equally important to those we regard as less sinful. Jesus befriended tax gatherers, prostitutes, and other unpopular sinners. He often ate with them, provoking much criticism from the hypocritical scribes and Pharisees (Luke 5:29-32; 7:34; 15:1-2; Matthew 9:10-13). Jesus stayed at the house of Zaccheus, a hated tax collector (Luke 19:1-9). The multitude that witnessed Zaccheus's reception of Jesus grumbled, "He has gone to be the guest of a man who is a sinner" (Luke 19:7). Jesus also approvingly permitted a woman who was apparently a notorious sinner to worship him by washing his feet with her tears and hair, kissing his feet, and anointing his feet with perfume (Luke 7:36-50). After his resurrection, Jesus first appeared to Mary Magdalene, from whom he had cast seven demons (Mark 16:9). Jesus' parable of the wedding feast summarizes well the equality of significance between the extremely sinful and the less sinful (Matthew 22:1-10). When the invited guests excuse themselves from coming, the king, who is also the bridegroom's father, opens the feast to everyone, "both evil and good" (Matthew 22:10).

Nor are the rich and powerful more important with God. By the same token the poor and lowly do not attract more of God's attention. God instructs Moses, "You shall do no injustice in judgment; you shall not be partial to the poor nor defer to the great, but you are to judge your neighbor fairly" (Leviticus 19:15; Exodus 23:3). The psalmist adds, "He will bless those who fear the LORD, the small together with the great" (Psalm 115:13). That no intrinsic difference separates one who happens to be a prince from one who happens to be poor is clear from Psalm 113:7-8:

> He raises the poor from the dust,
> And lifts the needy from the ash heap,
> To make them set with princes,
> With the princes of His people.

Accordingly, Nehemiah recognized that as governor he was no more important than his subjects: He refused the governor's larger food allowance (Nehemiah 5:14).

Too, with God, a slave is not less than a freeman. Paul says, in reference to the church of Christ, that "there is no distinction between . . . slave and freeman, but Christ is all, and in all" (Colossians 3:11).[10] But, looking from the other direction, neither is a slave more than his master. Jesus says, "A disciple is not above his teacher, nor a slave above his master. It is enough for the disciple that he become like his teacher, and the slave like his master" (Matthew 10:24-25).

It is consistent that Jesus gave no special regard to his earthly family (Luke 11:27-28; 8:19-21; Matthew 12:46-50). The same principle governs in the Old Testament, where God instructed Israel to treat the aliens or strangers as natives: "The stranger who resides with you shall be to you as the native among you, and you shall owe him as yourself; for you were aliens in the land of Egypt" (Leviticus 19:34; 15:14-15).

An illustration of the fact that God is not a respecter of persons comes from his frequent use of persons to perform tasks even though they appear to be unlikely and unsuited. God seldom uses the person whom we humans would choose. Indeed, "God choos[es] the poor of this world to be rich in faith and heirs of the kingdom" (James 2:5). He frequently used a barren womb to produce a person important in his plan of redemption. God used Sarah, Rebekah, Rachel, Hannah, and others in this way.[11]

Most of the leaders God has chosen would never have been chosen by men. Moses was "slow of speech and slow of tongue" (Exodus 4:10-12). He had no self-confidence, continually asking who would believe him. He lacked the smooth, fast tongue and self-assertiveness so essential for modern politicians. And Moses would seem further disqualified because he had never lived with his people. At the time God called him, Moses languished in exile in Midian for having killed an Egyptian. Yet he led the populous and rebellious nation of Israel on a forty-year trek through the desert to the land that God had promised Abraham's descendants.

God also used Gideon as his agent—this time to deliver Israel from the oppression of Midian. But Gideon was the youngest in his father's house, which ranked as the least in Mannaseh, and Gideon doubted God's miraculous power (Judges 6:11-15).

Jephthah is another unlikely character whom God made a leader. He was the son of a harlot and driven away from his father's house by his half-brothers (Judges 11:1-11). Nevertheless God used him to defeat the Ammonites who had attacked Israel.

David gives us a more familiar example. He was a shepherd boy and the youngest of eight sons whose own father couldn't imagine him as king (1 Samuel 16:5-13).

Jesus' apostles formed a most unlikely crew. Yet their Lord left them with the all-important tasks of spreading the gospel, writing the New Testament, and establishing the first-century church. As "uneducated and untrained men," Peter and John did not command human attention (Acts 4:13). Paul seemingly disqualified himself from leadership in the church by, as a member of the Sanhedrin, a history of passionately persecuting Christians. Paul stood unimpressive in appearance and, like Moses, lacked speaking ability (2 Corinthians 10:10).

Paul concludes that "God has chosen the foolish things of the world to shame the wise." In other words, "God has chosen the weak things of the world to shame the things which are strong, and the base things of the world and the despised God has chosen . . . so that no man may boast before God" (1 Corinthians 1:26-29).

But the ultimate instance of God's apparent preference for the unlikely person is the manner in which he himself visited this planet. Jesus Christ, the Almighty God of heaven, came as a servant—not a king. He was born to an obscure virgin girl in a stable (Luke 2:7). Jesus' Jewish neighbors rejected the testimony of His supernatural wisdom and miracles because they knew him and He seemed so ordinary. Matthew records:

> He came to His hometown and began teaching them in their synagogue, so that they became astonished, and said, "Where did this man get this wisdom and these miraculous powers? Is not this the carpenter's son? Is not His mother called Mary, and His brothers, James and Joseph and Simon and Judas? And His sisters, are they not all with us? Where then did this man get all these things?" And they took offense at Him. (Matthew 13:54-57)

God's use of the unlikely person demonstrates the equality of all people before him, which is an implication of his omniscience. In chapter 14, we will come back to the equality of all people.

As we shall see, under the teachings of Christianity, there remains still more to the significance of individual humans.

Questions for Reflection

1. What do the omniscience, omnipresence, and eternality of God add to individual human significance?

2. What scriptural references show that God is aware of every fact about every person, including all of his or her thoughts and actions?

3. Does God know more about each of us than we know about ourselves? What scriptural references support your answer?

4. Can you think of any scriptural references that show God is eternal and omnipresent? What do these references say?

5. If God is aware of every fact about every person, does a person add anything to his significance by trying to record and preserve his thoughts and actions? Why or why not?

6. Is God equally aware of every true fact, or does he know some better than others? What does this mean in terms of the significance of individual persons?

7. What biblical references show that God treats people equally or considers all people to be equally important?

8. What implications do you draw for individual human significance from the pattern of God choosing unlikely persons to further his redemptive plan?

9. God Interacts with Individual People

God . . . is a rewarder of those who seek Him.
—Hebrews 11:6

I am a flower quickly fading
Here today and gone tomorrow
A wave tossed in the ocean
Vapor in the wind
Still You hear me when I'm calling
Lord, You catch me when I'm falling
And You've told me who I am
I am Yours, I am Yours
— Casting Crowns, "Who Am I" (2003)

But the significance with God of individual persons does not stop with his omniscience. God does not serve merely as a cosmic tape recorder that passively sees and records everything that happens, though that by itself would be marvelous.

The third doctrine or teaching of Christianity that makes individual people important is that God reacts to the thoughts, words, and actions of humans. This stands as an important distinction between Christianity and other religions. Most other religions do not worship a personal god who interacts with human beings.

In his interactions with humans, some things please God and others displease him, though both are significant. In other words, there is a positive and negative significance. God's reactions to people issue from his character. God reigns not as a contentless observer of his universe but rather as a God with real preferences.

And God's character, and therefore preference, is holiness or righteousness. Scripture tells us over and over that God is holy (Leviticus 11:44; 19:1-2; 20:26; Joshua 24:18-19; 1 Samuel 2:2; Matthew 6:9). As Ezra says, "O LORD God of Israel, you are righteous!" (Ezra 9:15). The Bible also describes God's holiness as goodness. The Psalms are full of exhortations to praise God for his goodness: "Oh give thanks to the LORD, for He is good" (Psalm 106:1).[1] And Jesus affirms, "There is only One who is good" (Matthew 19:17). Jesus also describes God as "perfect" (Matthew 5:48).

God does not disregard his commandments (Matthew 5:17-18) or act contrary to his holy character (Numbers 22:19-20; Job 34:10). David says, "The LORD is righteous in all His ways" (Psalm 145:17). Indeed, "the LORD our God will have no part of unrighteousness or partiality or the taking of a bribe" (2 Chronicles 19:7).

Naturally, therefore, God is pleased to see people submit to his commandments and displeased to see them disobey his commandments. "I know, O my God, that You try the heart and delight in righteousness," David prays (1 Chronicles 29:17). On another occasion, David says, "He [God] loves righteousness and justice" (Psalm 33:5). God's distaste for evil is also expressed in Proverbs: "The way of the wicked is an abomination to the LORD, but He loves one who pursues righteousness" (Proverbs 15:9).[2] God's command to Judah well summarizes his pleasure in the righteousness of people and displeasure in their unrighteousness: "Cease to do evil, learn to do good" (Isaiah 1:16-17). In the New Testament, the theme repeats: "Abhor what is evil; cling to what is good" (Romans 12:9) and "flee from youthful lusts and pursue righteousness" (2 Timothy 2:22).

Thus, God's holiness serves as the basis of his response to people. God is pleased or displeased at every human thought, word, and deed. God also acts in response to them. He answers prayer, requites faith in him with eternal life, rewards righteousness, and punishes sin.

God Answers Prayer

The Bible promises that God will answer prayers asked by one who has faith that God answers and that are consistent with God's will. Proverbs says that "the desire of the righteous will be granted" (Proverbs 10:24). Jesus promises his disciples, "If you abide in Me, and My words abide in you, ask whatever you wish, and it will be done for you" (John 15:7). In other places Jesus assures his disciples that he will do anything asked in his name (John 14:13-14; 16:24; Mark 11:22-24). This includes moving mountains in response to prayer mixed with faith (Matthew 21:19-22; 6:5-7; 18:19-20; Mark 11:22-24).

The Bible overflows with specific instances of answered prayer. In response to prayers of distress, God often, for example, delivered Israel from bondage that he had imposed as punishment. Psalm 106:44-45 summarizes his deliverance:

> Nevertheless He looked upon their distress,
> When He heard their cry;
> And He remembered His covenant for their sake,
> And relented according to the greatness of His loving-kindness.

A good example of God's sparing Israel in response to prayer occurred when Israel had made a molten calf to worship at the same time that Moses was receiving the Ten Commandments from God on Mount Sinai. In response to prayer, "the LORD changed His mind about the harm which He said He would do to His people" (Exodus 32:9-12, 14).

God also frequently answers prayers for physical healing and well-being. In response to prayers, he opened the wombs of the household of Abimelech (Genesis 20:17-18), Rebekah (Genesis 25:21), and Elizabeth (Luke 1:11-13, 15-17, 24-25). Other examples of healing in answer to prayer are God's cleansing of Miriam from leprosy at the request of Moses (Numbers 12:9-15) and the restoring of the withered hand of Jeroboam at the petition of a "man of God" (1 Kings 13:4, 6).

Biblical accounts include God restoring life in response to prayer. For instance, God raised a widow's son from the dead upon Elijah's request (1 Kings 17:20-22). He also raised the dead son of a Shunamite woman at the request of Elisha (2 Kings 4:31-37). God gave fifteen years of additional life in response to Hezekiah's prayer (2 Kings 20:1-6).

Another general category of prayer that God answers is prayer for forgiveness of sin. We are told in the Psalms: "As for our transgressions, You forgive them" (Psalm 65:3).[3] But God does not automatically forgive. Forgiveness must be requested. David illustrates confession when he prays, "Acquit me of hidden faults" (Psalm 19:12). John makes forgiveness contingent on confession: "If we confess our sins, He is faithful and righteous to forgive us our sins and to cleanse us from all unrighteousness" (1 John 1:9). Solomon describes the process of forgiveness at the dedication of the temple when he asks God to forgive Israel whenever they confess and repent from sin (1 Kings 8:46-50). The reason that God is able to forgive is the vicarious death of Jesus Christ for man's sin.

A biblical example of God's forgiveness in response to a person's confession is the life of David, who committed both murder and adultery. After being confronted with his sin by Nathan the prophet, David confessed (2 Samuel 12:13; Psalm 51:2-14). After David's death, God says, "David . . . kept My commandments and . . . followed Me with all his heart, to do only that which was right in My sight" (1 Kings 14:8).[4] This is classic justification. David was treated as if he had never sinned.

Isaiah furnishes another example of God's forgiveness in response to man's petition. When Isaiah acknowledged that he was "a man of unclean lips," his "iniquity [was] taken away, and [his] sin [was] forgiven" (Isaiah 6:5-7).

The quantity of one's sin does not control God's ability to forgive. For example, Judah's sin of intermarriage with pagans reached such vast proportions that it could not all be confessed in one or two days, yet God forgave it (Ezra 10:13).

We have seen prayers for the deliverance of Israel, physical healing, and forgiveness answered in Scripture. But God has answered numerous and miscellaneous other prayers. He gave petitioners victory over enemies (2 Samuel 22:4-7, 18; 2 Chronicles 14:8-12; 18:31), protected (1 Chronicles 4:10; Ezra 8:21-23, 31), sent fire from heaven (1 Kings 18:36-38; 2 Kings 1:9-15), sent rain (1 Kings 18:42-45), provided drinking water (Judges 15:18-19), blinded an army (2 Kings 6:18), restored a kingdom (2 Chronicles 33:10-13), and sent an angel (Judges 13:8-11).

Kenneth N. Taylor notes that answers to prayers abound today: "Christians everywhere report that their prayers are answered. This is not generally true of devotees of other religions. It is apparently a phenomenon of Christianity."[5]

But generally God does not respond to the prayers of those who have not entered into a relationship with him through faith in Christ. Neither is God moved by the prayer of the believer in Christ who has wandered from fellowship with him. The psalmist says that God may refuse to answer a believer's prayer: "If I regard wickedness in my heart, the Lord will not hear" (Psalm 66:18). God's refusal to answer disobedient King Saul's prayers provides an example of this (1 Samuel 14:37; 28:5-6). The same theme rings in Deuteronomy, when Moses warned Israel that if they disobeyed God, "the heaven which is over your head shall be bronze, and the earth which is under you, iron" (Deuteronomy 28:23).

Nor does God answer prayers that are contrary to his will. God refused to answer Moses' plea that he be allowed to cross the Jordan with Israel (Deuteronomy 3:23-29), David's desperate prayer that the child born of his adulterous union with Bathsheba be spared (2 Samuel 12:14-18, 22), Job's prayer to be relieved of his affliction (Job 30:20), Paul's prayer that the thorn in the flesh be removed (2 Corinthians 12:7-9), and even Jesus' prayer repeated three times that he not have to suffer and die (Matthew 26:39, 42, 44).

But we must not infer from God's silence at certain prayers that he has not heard them. Silence serves as God's usual way of answering "no" or "wait," and we should not expect a miraculous presentation of that answer.

God Responds to Faith by Conferring Eternal Life

God also responds to individual people by requiting their faith in him with eternal life. If one believes that Jesus Christ is the Son of God and that he died and rose for the forgiveness of his sins, that person receives eternal life. This is the message of John 3:16: "For God so loved the world, that He gave His only begotten Son, that whoever believes in Him shall not perish, but have eternal life."[6]

God Rewards Righteousness

A third way God responds to human individuals is by rewarding righteousness—both in this life and in the life after death. We are told in Proverbs that "the righteous will be rewarded in the earth" (Proverbs 11:31). Jesus agrees that those who obey God will be blessed by God in their earthly lives (Mark 10:29-31). The writer of Hebrews says God "is a rewarder of those who seek Him" (Hebrews 11:6).

A revealing example is the series of promises God made to the Israelites before they crossed the Jordan. God promised that if Israel obeyed his commandments he would send rain and make the land productive (Leviticus 26:3-4; Deuteronomy 11:13-15; 28:12), bless the fruit of Israel's and the cattle's wombs (Deuteronomy 7:12-14; 28:4-5, 11-12), exalt Israel as a nation (Deuteronomy 15:6; 28:1, 9-10), and defeat Israel's enemies (Deuteronomy 28:7). Moses summarized, "And all these blessings shall come upon you and overtake you if you obey the LORD your God" (Deuteronomy 28:2).

God will also reward in heaven the righteous deeds of those who accept Christ as Savior. In other words, there is a benefit beyond eternal life that will be bestowed on the faithful when they reach heaven. Jesus told his disciples: "Rejoice and be glad, for your reward in heaven is great; for in the same way they persecuted the prophets who were before you" (Matthew 5:12). One way for a person to make treasure in heaven is by giving to the poor. Jesus instructed his disciples: "Sell your possessions and give to charity; make yourselves money belts which do not wear out, an unfailing treasure in heaven, where no thief comes near nor moth destroys" (Luke 12:33). Paul explains that fire will test the work of a Christian in order to determine his reward (1 Corinthians 3:11-15).

Heavenly rewards will take two forms. The first is tangible crowns. Paul said that he would receive such a crown as a reward for his faithfulness (2 Timothy 4:7-8).[7] The second kind of heavenly reward is position in heaven. For example, Jesus promised his disciples that they would "eat and drink at My table in My kingdom, and you will sit on thrones judging the twelve tribes of Israel" (Luke 22:28-30).[8]

God Punishes Sin

Another manner in which God responds to people is by punishing sin. Although we do not like to think about God punishing our sin, punishment affirms our individual significance.

The Bible repeatedly describes God as a God of vengeance: God cannot ignore man's unconfessed rebellion. God vows, "I will not acquit the guilty" (Exodus 23:7). He also declares, "I will punish the world for its evil and the wicked for their iniquity" (Isaiah 13:11). "Vengeance is Mine," he affirms (Deuteronomy 32:35). The apostle Paul adds that God's wrath will punish all of man's sin: "For the wrath of God is revealed from heaven against all ungodliness and unrighteousness of men who suppress the truth in unrighteousness" (Romans 1:18-19).[9] Jesus says, "Every careless word that people speak, they shall give an accounting for it in the day of judgment" (Matthew 12:36).

The antipathy of God toward evil is an expression of his holiness. He must react against and punish man's significant sin. As David says, "God is a righteous judge, and a God who has indignation every day" (Psalm 7:11). Isaiah explains that God's punishments overflow with righteousness: "A destruction is determined, overflowing with righteousness. For a complete destruction, one that is decreed, the LORD God of hosts will execute in the midst of the whole land" (Isaiah 10:22-23). Isaiah adds, "But the LORD of hosts will be exalted in judgment" (Isaiah 5:16). God's holiness, which summarizes his immutable character, establishes the absolute of the universe. As such, it forms a large "stone to strike and a rock to stumble over" (Isaiah 8:13-15).

God's judgments also cannot be escaped. A man may successfully flee the jurisdiction of a human court or resist the constable, but the judgments of the omnipotent God will be enforced

(1 Samuel 2:9-10). Isaiah agrees that human strength cannot mount a defense to God:

> The strong man will become tinder,
> His work also a spark.
> Thus they shall both burn together,
> And there will be none to quench them. (Isaiah 1:31)

God's vengeance is not arbitrary or capricious. God responds to evil in accordance with his character and holiness. Isaiah says of Judah,

> Woe to them!
> For they have brought evil on themselves. . . .
> Woe to the wicked! It will go badly with him,
> For what he deserves will be done to him. (Isaiah 3:9-11)

God is a just God. David says, "For the LORD loves justice" (Psalm 37:28). David adds,

> Against You, You only, I have sinned
> And done what is evil in Your sight,
> So that You are justified when You speak
> And blameless when You judge. (Psalm 51:4)

Moses affirms that God is just:

> Ascribe greatness to our God!
> "The Rock! His work is perfect,

> For all His ways are just;
> A God of faithfulness and without injustice,
> Righteous and upright is He." (Deuteronomy 32:3-4)[10]

The Bible warns repeatedly that God punishes those who disobey him. An enlightening illustration is God's dealing with Israel. Before Israel crossed the Jordan into Canaan, God instructed the Israelites to drive out the Canaanite nations, having nothing to do with their foreign gods (Exodus 23:23; Deuteronomy 9:3-4; 20:17-18). Joshua repeated this warning on the other side of the Jordan: "If you forsake the LORD and serve foreign gods, then He will turn and do you harm and consume you after He has done good to you" (Joshua 24:20).

There are also many examples of God carrying out his warnings and punishing the sin of human individuals. When Adam and Eve ate of the forbidden tree, God cursed them and the world (Genesis 3). When all people but Noah became corrupt, all were drowned except Noah, his family, and a single pair of each animal species (Genesis 6–8). The most abundant source of examples is once again God's dealings with Israel. When Israel as God's instrument of justice became wicked, God refused to drive out the Canaanites (Judges 2:20-23). God also punished Israel's sin by causing it to be defeated in battle (Psalm 78:62).[11] Too, God often delivered Israel into bondage under its enemies.[12] God also punished Israel through disease,[13] famine,[14] and in other ways.[15]

Human sin is so significant that God even afflicts nature because of it (Genesis 3:17-18). He cursed the ground because of Adam's sin and destroyed most animal life in the flood because of man's great wickedness (Genesis 7:17, 21-23). God often destroyed the productivity of the land in judgment (Psalm 107:33).[16]

The most sobering punishment that God imposes is hell. According to Jesus, hell is a place of outer darkness (Matthew 8:12; 25:30), pain (Matthew 8:12), unquenchable fire (Matthew 25:41), and tears (Matthew 22:10-14). It never becomes tolerable or ends (Matthew 25:41). The Bible teaches that people live eternally after death in either heaven or hell and that hell is the place to which those who don't believe in Christ are consigned (John 3:36).

Jesus Christ endured every person's hell in the ultimate expression of God's vengeance (Psalm 16:10; Acts 2:27, 31). God poured out his wrath against all of our sins on his Son Jesus. As Paul explains, "He [God] made Him [Jesus] who knew no sin to be sin on our behalf, so that we might become the righteousness of God in Him" (2 Corinthians 5:21).[17]

To one who accepts Christ's payment for his sin, God's treatment of his sin takes the form of chastisement. The believer's sin is forgiven, but God still reacts with chastening in order to uproot habitual sin. The psalmist, for example, says, "The LORD has disciplined me severely, but He has not given me over to death" (Psalm 118:18). In the New

Testament, Paul was afflicted with an unnamed physical ailment that God used to control his pride (2 Corinthians 12:7-10).

This chastening should ultimately be regarded as a comfort. That God is concerned enough about one person to seek to change him is indeed reason to rejoice. David expresses this same thought: "Your rod and Your staff, they comfort me" (Psalm 23:4).

At first glance it may appear quite unkind for God to punish our sin. However, the failure of God to punish our sin would negate our dignity and significance. Because every detail of the life of every person is significant, her sin cannot be ignored. If human misdeeds were not allowed to incur their natural consequences (i.e., judgment and punishment), each of us, as an individual, would be a zero, a nothing. We would not be significant. It would be infinitely more cruel for God to pretend, if that were even possible, that humans are good. So even the unrepentant person can take comfort in knowing that he at least has significance. No matter how wicked a person is, God still knows him exhaustively and reacts to his deeds. He does not merely slip away like a dissipating puff of smoke.

Therefore, God's vengeance should be an item of praise. We should rejoice that God respects human choices. Fittingly, Moses calls on all nations to rejoice in God's wrath:

> "Rejoice, O nations, with His people;
> For He will avenge the blood of His servants,
> And will render vengeance on His adversaries,

And will atone for His land and His people."
(Deuteronomy 32:43)

The Psalms direct all creation in a song of joy over God's judgment:

> Let the heavens be glad, and let the earth rejoice;
> Let the sea roar, and all it contains.
> Then all the trees of the forest will sing for joy,
> Before the LORD, for He is coming,
> For He is coming to judge the earth.
> He will judge the world in righteousness,
> And the peoples in His faithfulness. (Psalm 96:11-13)[18]

Thus, God's practice of responding to individual people adds to our significance. As we will see next, a final Christian teaching that makes the individual significant is the immortality of every person.

Questions for Reflection

1. Does our significance stop with each of us being made in God's image and God knowing us exhaustively? What Scriptures support your answer?

2. Does God interact with individual persons and, if so, how?

3. What does Scripture teach about God's interaction with individual people?

4. Do you believe that God hears and responds to your prayers? Why or why not?

5. If a request stated in a prayer is not granted, what might that mean?

6. Does the Bible teach that there are any conditions for effective prayer? If so, what are they?

7. According to the Bible, how does a person receive salvation, or eternal life from God?

8. How does God reward righteousness and punish sin? Are his judgments just? What scriptural references support your answer?

9. What actions of individual persons receive God's reward? What actions incur his punishment?

10. People Live Forever After Death

But we do not want you to be uninformed, brethren, about those who are asleep, that you may not grieve, as do the rest who have no hope. For if we believe that Jesus died and rose again, even so God will bring with Him those who have fallen asleep in Jesus. . . . Therefore comfort one another with these words.

—1 Thessalonians 4:13-14, 18

We have seen that—according to the doctrines of Christianity—God made each of us in his image, knows all about us, and responds to us. But if this is all there is to our importance, we could still be unhappy, because death, what Albert Camus calls "the densest silence of all,"[1] would remain. Despite the fullness of my significance during my earthly life, I would remain dreadfully small if my existence ceases when I die. But, according to the teachings of Christianity,

> this perishable must put on the imperishable, and this mortal must put on immortality. But when this perishable will have put on the imperishable, and this mortal will have put on immortality, then will come about the saying that is written, "DEATH IS SWALLOWED UP in victory. O DEATH, WHERE IS YOUR VICTORY? O DEATH, WHERE IS YOUR STING?" The sting of death is sin, and the power of sin is the law; but thanks be to God, who gives us the victory through our Lord Jesus Christ. (1 Corinthians 15:53-57)

As incredible as it seems, there remains more to individual human significance than the image of God, his knowledge of every person, and his interactions with us. Death does not reduce a person to a mere memory of God when one's seventy years on earth are spent. Rather, a person lives on after death. Yes, individual humans are immortal. Every person receives an eternity to see and appreciate his significance. Job asks the time-honored question and then answers it:

> "If a man dies, will he live again?
> All the days of my struggle I will wait
> until my change comes.
> "You will call, and I will answer You;
> You will long for the work of Your hands." (Job 14:14-15)

The writer of Ecclesiastes concurs in Job's answer: "For man goes to his eternal home while mourners go about in the street" (Ecclesiastes 12:5).[2]

Biblical teachings on immortality include the notion that the physical body of every person, in addition to her soul or spirit, will live forever. Jesus teaches that a person will enter eternity in her body (Matthew 18:8-9). Recall that Moses and Elijah, who had been dead for centuries, appeared in their bodies with Jesus at his transfiguration, and the rich man recognized Abraham and Lazarus in heaven (Luke 16:19-31). In John 5:28-29, Jesus explicitly teaches a bodily resurrection of all dead: "An hour is coming, in which all who are in the tombs will hear His voice, and will come forth; those who did the good deeds to a resurrection of life, those who committed the evil deeds to a resurrection of judgment."

Paul emphatically proclaims the stunning news of the Christian's physical resurrection. In one passage, he says:

> For this we say to you by the word of the Lord, that we who are alive and remain until the coming of the Lord, will not precede those who have fallen asleep. For the Lord Himself will descend from heaven with a shout, with the voice of the archangel and with the trumpet of God, and the dead in Christ shall rise first. Then we who are alive and remain shall be caught up together with them in the clouds to meet the Lord in the air, and so we shall always be with the Lord. Therefore comfort one another with these words. (1 Thessalonians 4:15-18)

C. S. Lewis, emphasizing the importance of the individual and his immortality in Christian doctrine, writes that "the individual person will outlive the universe." He continues, "There will come a time when every culture, every institution, every nation, the human race, all biological life is extinct and every one of us is still alive." Lewis adds, "If we do not believe it, let us be honest and relegate the Christian faith to museums."[3]

Christian Scripture teaches that the afterlife stands both as an extension and a consequence of the present life. There are two post-death realms, heaven and hell, and one's particular destination depends on his acceptance or rejection of Jesus Christ in the present life

(Matthew 25:41, 46; John 3:15-16, 36). Therefore, one's eternal significance carries a positive or negative character.

Most philosophers and theologians have had their say on the question of life after death. Process theologian Charles Hartshorne has explored this subject, and his views provide a window for understanding more fully the Christian doctrine of individual human immortality. Hartshorne argues in *The Logic of Perfection* that people cease to exist at death, yet God's omniscience of them after death provides a meaningful and satisfactory everlasting life. But is this really a satisfactory form of immortality?

Hartshorne, after saying that people cease to exist at death, hedges by insisting that death is not destruction. He distinguishes the status of a person before birth (i.e., nonexistence) from his status after death (i.e., he can still be referred to or talked about). For Hartshorne, this referability after death provides a form of continued existence:

> If we drop this impossible extreme [only as something happens can it be referred to], then we must also break once for all with the idea of death as simple destruction of an individual. An individual becomes, he does not de-become or unbecome; he is created, he is not destroyed or de-created.[4]

Hartshorne appeals to process theology in making his point. He explains that "becoming" contains "being," so that being is never eradicated but merely incorporated into "becoming" novel states of total reality. In other words, the same matter and energy in the universe today ("being") will still be there tomorrow ("becoming"), although it will not be in the same form. This resembles New Age thinking and the monistic theme of Eastern religions: Individual humans (to the extent there really is a self) are not destroyed by death but are absorbed into and preserved in future states of reality or the monistic whole.

How do we answer this? Although matter and energy are conserved from the present into the future, their present arrangement is certainly lost in "becoming." And individual persons are arrangements or bundles of particles that undergo destruction if there is no life after death. Further, blurring the distinction between what is here today ("being") and what will be here tomorrow ("becoming") cheats what is real. The present is real; the future is not. There is dramatic and often sorrowful change when the present gives way to "becoming." Ask yourself whether a real change occurs when a previously healthy, happy young person is suddenly killed in a car accident. It is scant comfort that the particles in his body exist in other forms after his death.

Moreover, the fact that the events of the past can be referred to today does not make them any more presently real than the unknown future. The memory of something does not affect its actual existence. Thus, in spite of Hartshorne's hedging, under his view, people—as they die—cease to exist in reality. Consciousness ceases at death.

So, what sort of survival is offered people by a system like this? Hartshorne answers that all of the thoughts, feelings, and actions

139

of every individual person are preserved in God's memory and God is constantly aware of each piece of information. And, Hartshorne adds, God reforms his awareness of us forever.[5]

But, under Hartshorne's position, the following are losses suffered by an individual person at his death:

- consciousness,
- the possibility of making new memories,
- the ability to remember,
- the ability to be aware of and enjoy the fact that one is remembered by God and by others,
- the ability to be aware of and appreciate the continuing impact of one's pre-death actions, and
- the possibility of seeing evil ultimately corrected.

All of these features of life, which are desirable, are concluded by death—under this view. Hartshorne says, "Death is the last page of the last chapter of the book of one's life."[6] In fact, Hartshorne's vision is little different from the view expressed in *Humanist Manifesto II* that people experience life after death only "in our progeny and in the way that our lives have influenced others in our culture."[7]

In summary, four teachings of Christianity combine to give each individual person as much significance or importance as it is possible for him to have. These teachings are:

1. God has created each individual human is his image,
2. the omnipresent, eternal, and omniscient God is fully aware of every person,
3. this same God responds to each person, and
4. every person lives forever after death.

None of us could be any more significant than each of us is now or will be at all times in the future. Each of us is or will be completely known, appreciated, influential, and remembered. In the remaining chapters, we'll explore the consequences of the significance accorded by Christianity to the individual person.

Questions for Reflection

1. Does individual human significance consist of any more than a person being made in God's image, God knowing him exhaustively, and God interacting with him? What scriptural references can you find to support your answer?

2. How does the Christian teaching of the immortality of each human being add to our individual significance?

3. Does the Christian doctrine of immortality include the survival of the individual person's physical body? What importance does that have to you?

4. Does the clear New Testament teaching of life after death shed light on Old Testament passages touching on this subject? If so, how?

5. If a person could assure that he would be remembered by other people, would that be as good as life after death? Why or why not?

6. What benefits does eternal life offer to an individual over annihilation accompanied by the possibility of being remembered by other persons?

7. If there is no life after death but God remembers us, is that a satisfying substitute for immortality? Why or why not?

8. Would it be kind or generous for God to annihilate people who choose permanently to reject him? What scriptural references support your answer?

Section III:
The Consequences of the Significance
of the Individual Person

11. Individual Human Significance Is Complete

It is a serious thing to live in a society of possible gods and goddesses, to remember that the dullest and most uninteresting person you talk to may one day be a creature which, if you saw it now, you would strongly be tempted to worship, or else a horror and a corruption such as you now meet, if at all, only in a nightmare. All day long we are, in some degree, helping each other to one or other of these destinations. It is in the light of these overwhelming possibilities, it is with the awe and the circumspection proper to them, that we should conduct all our dealings with one another, all friendships, all loves, all play, all politics. There are no ordinary people. You have never talked to a mere mortal.

—C. S. Lewis, *The Weight of Glory*[1]

L et's focus now on the consequences of the truth of individual human significance. How do these Christian doctrines elaborate into our lives? In other words, how should a person in possession of the truth about the significance of individual humans act or think differently?

The basic fact is that individual human significance stands complete or as great as it could ever be regardless of one's accomplishments or status. It cannot, therefore, be decreased or increased. Because a person's significance does not consist in his carving a niche in history, the pressure is off. We are not slipping away unnoticed. And there is no such thing as a threat to our significance.

Jesus' words in Matthew 10:30-31 provide great comfort: "The very hairs of your head are all numbered. So do not fear." The writer of Hebrews assures us, "God is not unjust so as to forget your work and the love which you have shown toward His name, in having ministered and in still ministering to the saints" (Hebrews 6:10). Paul adds that he is "fully known" by God, which he will someday understand (1 Corinthians 13:12), and that he is "well known to God" (2 Corinthians 5:11 NKJV).

The Tomb of the Unknowns at Arlington National Cemetery bears this inscription: "Here rests in honored glory an American soldier known but to God." This inscription expresses our sincere hope and belief that God knows what we do not and cannot know about ourselves and each other—in this case the identity of an otherwise unidentified body.

Because God knows who each of us is, we can relax—regardless of the human attention we command. When questions as to our significance arise, which will happen in an unfathomably large universe where a planet containing more than seven billion people is but a tiny particle, we should not think of our accomplishments, compliments we have received, or abilities. Rather, we can think about the fact that we are constructed in God's image, are objects of God's omniscience and response, and are immortal.

Moreover, the number of human minds that are aware of a fact has nothing to do with that fact's significance. Events unwitnessed by any human senses, as the frantic thoughts of a forgotten man lost in the wilderness, stand just as significant as if a million people were aware of them. Because of God's complete knowledge, being the best at something commands no more significance than being second best. Bill is not less than Tom because Tom can play ping-pong better than Bill can. The silver medalist is not less significant than the gold medal winner.

One of the best-known names in history is Alexander Graham Bell, who patented the telephone. Almost no one knows the name of Bell's contemporary Elisha Gray. But Gray invented the telephone at the same time as Bell, and some say he invented the device first. Gray, however, reached the patent office on February 14, 1876, two hours after Bell.[2] Although major corporations have carried the name of Bell and his name is seen and repeated thousands of times every day, the forgotten Gray stands equally significant to Bell, according to the Christian view of human significance.

We all know of the midnight ride of Paul Revere, who warned American patriots in April 1775, "The British are coming." But few of us know of William Dawes. Riding over the same route and on the same night as Revere, Dawes carried the same warning about British movements. Revere is memorialized in Henry Wadsworth Longfellow's famous poem "Paul Revere's Ride," but Dawes, who is not the subject of such a poem, is forgotten.[3] Under the truths of Christianity, however, Hawes carries equal significance to Revere, despite Hawes's lack of fame.

In the movie *On the Waterfront* (1954), Marlon Brando's character, Terry, captures all of our fears with these memorable lines: "You don't understand. I coulda had class, I coulda been a contender. I coulda been somebody, instead of a bum, which is what I am, let's face it." Christianity says that all of us, whether recognized by others as a contender or not and whether we have class or not, are fully significant. No matter how obscure we feel, nothing would be added to our significance if we were recognized by the whole world as "contenders" with "class."

Therefore, nothing can shake our worth, and nothing should cause us to fret over what we might have been but for some unfavorable circumstance. There is nothing lost if we had the latent ability to be good or great at something but never developed that ability. God knows latent abilities as well as developed skills. God knows who won the tennis tournament as well as those who could have won had they entered. The truth of individual human significance gives us reason to accept ourselves as we are. Our importance does not depend on doing something nobody else has ever done or becoming the world's best at something. In the words of one writer, "By affirming God's truth about our worth, we will lodge it deep within our hearts and minds and begin to reshape our thinking, feelings, and behavior."[4]

We should learn from Jesus' sharp disapproval of the disciples' discussing who was the greatest:

> And there arose also a dispute among them as to which one of them was regarded to be the greatest. And He said to them, "The kings of the Gentiles lord it over them; and those who have authority over them are called 'Benefactors.' But not so with you, but let him who is the greatest among you become as the youngest, and the leader as the servant. For who is greater, the one who reclines at table, or the one who serves? Is not the one who reclines at table? But I am among you as the one who serves." (Luke 22:24-27)

Therefore, Christians, because they more than non-Christians should appreciate man's true significance, have no reason to hold contests to uncover, for example, the best soul-winner or preacher.

One can add nothing to her significance by impressing, or getting the attention of, other people. Our identity rests in God, not in the impressions we forge in the finite minds of others or the number of times they repeat our names. Consequently, there is no point in detailing my accomplishments to you for the mere purpose of being noticed. When he felt disrespected, the biblical character Haman, as recorded in Esther and mentioned earlier in this book, recited his accomplishments and status: "Haman recounted to them the glory of his riches, and the number of his sons, and every instance where the king had magnified him, and how he had promoted him above the princes and servants of the king" (Esther 5:11). But, as Haman admitted, "all of this does not satisfy me" (Esther 5:13). The all-too-human bragging by Haman was futile and pointless.

I don't need to write letters or send tweets for the bare purpose of letting others know what I am doing or every thought I have. Proverbs says, "A fool does not delight in understanding, but only in revealing his own mind" (Proverbs 18:2). Consider too that Jesus often remained silent.[5] He didn't, for example, tell the poor widow who gave all she had of his approval (Mark 12:41-44). But she stands fully significant, no less than if her actions had been commemorated by a monument or written record of her name.

This truth of individual human significance means that one can use his second-best china without telling his guests that he has better or permit others to think that he knows less about a subject than he does. It is not a tragedy if no one knows that I am responsible for some benefit that another person enjoys. I don't need to tell my roommates when I clean up the apartment or sound a trumpet when I cut the grass. It is even endurable for another to get the credit for what I have accomplished.

The irrelevance of promoting is also plain from the manner in which God appeared in the person of Jesus. He was totally unglamorous. He did not come with royal pomp but rather slipped into the world through a Bethlehem stable. On his day of greatest human glory, he rode into town on a borrowed donkey. He was ordinary looking, with practically no possessions and only a few ignorant followers who had no pedigree.

Questions for Reflection

1. On what does individual human significance ultimately depend?

2. Can a person add to his significance by seeking the attention of other people and being remembered by them? Give reasons for your response.

3. Does disrespect by other people threaten a person's significance? Why or why not?

4. What do Jesus' words in Matthew 10:30-31 say about the importance of the individual person?

5. A Sunday school chorus begins "Do Lord, O do Lord, O do remember me." Under the teachings of Christianity, is there any chance that God will forget you? What scriptural references support your answer?

6. Did the seemingly impressive achievements (prestige, money, status, and family) of the Old Testament character Haman satisfy him? Do similar accomplishments of people today satisfy them? Why or why not?

12. Length of Life Does Not Affect the Significance of a Person

For a day in Your courts is better than a thousand outside.
—Psalm 84:10

The completeness of individual human significance means that a short life enjoys no less significance than a long one. A person who dies as an infant and a person who lives to be eighty or ninety years old are equally made in God's image, known by God, reacted to by God, and immortal. On these criteria, it makes no difference how many times one rides the earth around the sun. These principles should help those who struggle with the loss of a family member at a young age. Death at any age is difficult to accept, and premature death is especially devastating to a bereaved family.

But the length of a human life does not determine its significance. As we are told in the Psalms, "For a day in Your courts is better than a thousand outside" (Psalm 84:10). Although it may not be better, a short life *outside* of God's courts is, under the principles of significance, also no less significant than a long life. Remember, even one who is not a follower of Christ carries God's image, is known by God, reacted to by him, and immortal.

The sentiments of English poet Ben Johnson deliver powerful insight. He recognizes that mere length of life does not confer merit and a short life may in fact be more praiseworthy than a long one:

> It is not growing like a tree
> In bulk, doth make Man better be;
> Or standing long an oak, three hundred year,
> To fall a log at last, dry, bald, and sere:
> A lily of a day
> Is fairer far in May,
> Although it fall and die that night—
> It was the plant and flower of light.
> In small proportions we just beauties see;
> And in short measures life may perfect be.[1]

Under the truths of Christianity, a short life is always equally significant as a long one.

Indeed, a brief or once-repeated experience may, on the principles of true significance, prove as satisfying as one that, at least in human terms, is long-lasting. Why do we automatically think that it is superior to have been to Paris twenty-five times, as opposed to once? Both numbers are finite, and both sets of experiences can be equally held in the mind of the person who has lived them. In fact, the person who has visited Paris once may more vividly remember and cherish her experience than the one who has been there twenty-five times. More importantly, both sets of experiences are equally known by God. And each set is eclipsed by the infinite length of life that opens before every one of us.

Due to our fear of insignificance, we clutch the ephemeral present. But the effort is futile. Recognizing that individual human significance flows from the nature and actions of God frees us to enjoy the moment without futilely trying to prolong or freeze it (as through photography or souvenir mania). William Blake captured the freedom of releasing the nonce:

> He who binds to himself a joy
> Does the winged life destroy;
> But he who kisses joy as it flies
> Lives in eternity's sunrise.[2]

Recognition of the true source of individual human significance removes the sting from our earthly transience. According to the teachings of Christianity, Christ's resurrection has defeated the ancient human foe, death: "O DEATH, WHERE IS YOUR VICTORY? O DEATH, WHERE IS YOUR STING?" (1 Corinthians 15:55).

One who lives a short life on this earth is no less immortal than one who lives what we consider a long life here. There are no degrees of immortality. Every human life is infinite in length.

Questions for Reflection

1. Psalm 84:10 says that "a day in [God's] courts is better than a thousand outside." What are the implications of this truth for the significance of an individual person?

2. Under the teachings of Christianity, is a person who dies young less immortal and less significant than a person who lives a long life?

3. Are there degrees of immortality or is every human life infinite in length?

4. Is there any comfort for a grieving family in the Christian teaching of the immortality of every human life?

13. Popularity Is of No Account

For the growing good of the world is partly dependent on unhistoric acts; and that things are not so ill with you and me as they might have been, is half owing to the number who lived faithfully a hidden life, and rest in unvisited tombs.
—George Eliot, *Middlemarch*[1]

A person's significance is not a function of his popularity among other people. Consider the person who spends his life in seclusion on a small island in the Pacific—as the handful of Japanese soldiers who, years after World War II, were found hiding in the jungles, unaware of the war's end.[2] Compare a person who is instantly recognized on worldwide television or whose name is known to everyone, such as Abraham Lincoln[3] or George Washington.[4] According to Christian teachings, they are all fully and equally significant because each is made in God's image, God is completely aware of each, God responds to each, and each enjoys immortality.

So there is no need to be a collector of friends. There is no reason to meet as many people as I possibly can and make sure that I get more phone calls and letters than you do. One need not troll social media sites on the Internet in order to collect more "friends" or "contacts" than others.

Neither should it bother us that our friends have just as much fun when we are not around or that no one remembers our birthdays, unless this reflects improper attitudes or behavior on our part. So what if the professor doesn't know my name! So what if you receive more compliments or have more Facebook friends than I! Even if I am so obscure that no one could identify my body if I fell dead on the street in front of my house tomorrow, I am just as significant as Napoleon at the height of his power. In other words, the persons buried in potters' fields and the illiterate ragpickers from the lowest caste or subcaste in India (such as the Dalits, or untouchables) are no less significant than the most celebrated presidents of the United States— Lincoln, Franklin Roosevelt, Kennedy, and Reagan—whose funeral processions drew vast throngs of mourners.

One person who has ironically become almost famous for his obscurity is Elmer McCurdy. He was a laughably incompetent outlaw from Oklahoma who botched a train robbery in 1911 and was killed a short time later in a shootout, after vowing not to be taken alive. When his body went unclaimed at the funeral home, the undertaker mummified it and charged a nickel (placed in McCurdy's mouth) for each curiosity seeker who wished to view the corpse. Its identity forgotten, the body was then featured over many years in a string of carnivals, wax museums, and haunted houses. Eventually, the corpse reached "The Laff in the Dark" funhouse at the Long Beach Pike amusement park in California. During the filming of a television episode in 1976, a crew member was moving what was thought to be a wax mannequin hanging from a gallows. When the mannequin's arm broke off, it was discovered that the remains were human. Through various clues and newspaper accounts, police and researchers later identified the body as McCurdy's.[5] Under the teachings of Christianity, McCurdy stands no less significant (even when his body was thought to be a wax mannequin) than if he had been a truly famous and respected historical character.

The same is true of "John Doe No. 1." In July 2002, a man was exercising at a high school stadium in Atlanta. Carrying no identification, he slipped and fell, striking his head. He was rushed to a local hospital with a traumatic brain injury. Almost four years later, he remained in custodial care in a persistent vegetative state. He could smile and follow people with his eyes but could not speak or feed himself. He could not explain who he was, and no one was able to identify him. No spouse, no partner, no relative, no friend.[6] Yet, if we accept the teachings of Christianity, John Doe No. 1 has no less significance than George Washington.

Jesus was not concerned about his popularity. He said on one occasion, "I do not receive glory from men" (John 5:41). In fact, Jesus disregarded human traditions. He healed on the Sabbath, incurring much disfavor (Mark 3:1-6). He associated with disliked people, thus sharing their unpopularity (Luke 7:33-35).

One may play an important role and yet not be recognized or identified by any other human being. In other words, one's identity may be unknown or forgotten by all other people. The widow, whom Jesus commended in Mark 12:41-44 for giving only one cent at the temple (but all that she had), has set an enduring example of Christian sacrifice and stewardship. Yet no human alive today knows her identity. The same is true of the four men who let the paralytic down through the roof in order to reach Jesus when he was in Capernaum (Mark 2:1-12). Moreover, no one knows the identity of the boy whose five loaves and two small fish fed five thousand men, plus women and children (John 6:1-13). Numerous skilled craftsmen worked on the tabernacle, temple, and wall of Jerusalem. Most of them are not identified and stand forgotten to human history.[7] Yet all of these unknown persons are known to God and are no less significant than if their names were prominent in world history. This is so because each is made in God's image, exhaustively known by God, responded to by him, and each will live forever.

So we need not be like the biblical character Diotrephes, whom the apostle John criticized because he "love[d] to be first among them" (3 John 9). I don't need to be recognized as first or run around trying to get attention. The number of sheets of paper or electronic files with my name on them stored away in filing cabinets or on computer storage media someplace has nothing to do with my real significance. God's omniscience gives me all the attention I can handle. Each of us enjoys complete significance on the dark side of Pluto right now because the omnipresent God is there responding to each of us, and we can add nothing to our importance by going there and erecting a four-hundred-foot obelisk with our names carved on it. We can be content doing what appear to be small things. We can cheerfully comply with the direction against "seeking great things for yourself" (Jeremiah 45:5).[8]

But the irrelevance of fame or renown to true significance does not mean that it is of no use at all. For example, God gave Solomon fame: "And the LORD highly exalted Solomon in the sight of all Israel, and bestowed on him royal majesty which had not been on any king before him in Israel" (1 Chronicles 29:25). Solomon's wisdom was known not just in Israel but also in all the surrounding nations (1 Kings 4:31). Because of his fame "men came from all peoples to hear the wisdom of Solomon, from all the kings of the earth who had heard of his wisdom" (1 Kings 4:34). Those who came included the queen of Sheba. This enabled Solomon to answer her questions about God:

> Now when the queen of Sheba heard about the fame of Solomon concerning the name of the LORD, she came to test him with difficult questions. . . . When she came to Solomon, she spoke with him about all that was in her heart. And Solomon answered all her questions: nothing was hidden from the king which he did not explain to her. (1 Kings 10:1-3)

But the fame that drew the queen of Sheba to Solomon was "concerning the name of the LORD"—it was not just about Solomon himself. God also gave useful fame to Joshua (Joshua 3:7; 6:27) and David (2 Samuel 7:9).

By the same token, a Christian should be careful not to make his spiritual activities plays for personal attention. There is usually no advantage—and it may be spiritually harmful—to make sure other people know how much one prays, memorizes Scripture, gives, or fasts. Jesus warned his disciples, "Beware of practicing your righteousness before men to be noticed by them; otherwise you have no reward with your Father who is in heaven" (Matthew 6:1). Jesus went on to specify acts that should be conducted without thought of how many people are watching:

> "So when you give to the poor, do not sound a trumpet before you, as the hypocrites do in the synagogues and in the streets, so that they may be honored by men. Truly I say to you, they have their reward in full. But when you give to the poor, do not let your left hand know what your right hand is doing, so that your giving will be in secret; and your Father who sees what is done in secret will reward you.

> "When you pray, you are not to be like the hypocrites; for they love to stand and pray in the synagogues and on the street corners, so that they may be seen by men. Truly I say to you, they have their reward in full. But you, when you pray, go into your inner room, close your door and pray to your Father who is in secret, and your Father who sees what is done in secret will reward you.

> "And when you are praying, do not use meaningless repetition as the Gentiles do, for they suppose that they will be heard for their many words. . . .

"Whenever you fast, do not put on a gloomy face as the hypocrites do, for they neglect their appearance so that they will be noticed by men when they are fasting. Truly I say to you, they have their reward in full. But you, when you fast, anoint your head, and wash your face so that your fasting will not be noticed by men, but by your Father who is in secret; and your Father who sees what is done in secret will reward you. (Matthew 6:2-7, 16-18)

Charitable giving, prayer, and fasting do not depend for their effectiveness on the number of human observers.

This does not mean, however, that a Christian should hide all his accomplishments and never mention himself. A Christian author might, for example, legitimately list her degrees in order to gain a hearing. But she should test her motives. Laudable motives for a Christian to talk about her accomplishments include witnessing to non-Christians, encouraging Christians in their faith, and otherwise glorifying God. Newsletters sharing prayer requests are a helpful form of communication, for instance.

A biblical example of the useful reporting of accomplishments is King David telling the people of Israel what he had given for the construction of the temple before he asked them to give. "Then King David said to the entire assembly, . . . 'Now with all my ability I have provided for the house of my God. . . . Who then is willing to consecrate himself this day to the LORD?' " (1 Chronicles 29:1-2, 5). Paul and his missionary companions were careful to report their missionary successes to other believers (Acts 14:25-28; 15:2-4; 21:17-20). Paul even went so far as to advise the Christians in the various churches to imitate him (1 Corinthians 4:16-17; 11:1-2).[9] But Paul's motive was to see them grow to Christian maturity, not to make a name for himself.

In calling attention to oneself, as in everything else, a Christian should do "all in the name of the Lord Jesus" (Colossians 3:17).[10] The goal should be to be please God and be known by him, not to please others and be known by them. As Paul says, "If anyone loves God, he is known by Him" (1 Corinthians 8:3).

Fame may be like money. It can be useful but one should not seek or "love" it. Remember, it is not money itself but the "love of money" that is the root of all evil (I Timothy 6:10). In the same way, the sin of the scribes and Pharisees was not in having human attention but in seeking it (Matthew 23:5). The temptation to seek or love money and fame for their own sakes is so intoxicating that few can resist it. Resisting it may be, in Jesus' words, like trying to push a "camel . . . through the eye of a needle." (Matthew 19:24).

Questions for Reflection

1. Are unknown persons buried in unmarked graves around the world as significant as Abraham Lincoln, one of the most famous Americans of all time? Why or why not?

2. Are poor, unknown, powerless people living today less significant than rich, famous, powerful persons? Why or why not?

3. According to the teachings of Christianity, are all persons equally made in God's image, known to God, subjects of interaction with him, and immortal? What does this say about the equality of their significance?

4. Can you increase your significance by gaining fame or popularity? How would you explain your answer?

5. Is there any reason to seek the attention of other people when making donations, praying, and fasting? How might seeking human attention undermine the purpose of these activities, which is to glorify God?

6. Compare the significance of persons who willingly labor for God's kingdom on remote mission fields or in other unnoticed

roles with that of preachers who dazzle large television audiences.

7. Can fame be used for God's glory, instead of personal gratification? How did Solomon use his fame?

8. How did David publicly use his example of giving to spur the Israelites to support the construction of the temple?

9. In urging others to imitate him, what was Paul's motive?

14. Treat People Equally

"YOU SHALL LOVE YOUR NEIGHBOR AS YOURSELF."
— Matthew 19:19

There is neither Jew nor Greek, there is neither slave nor free man, there is neither male nor female; for you are all one in Christ Jesus.
— Galatians 3:28

A related consequence of the truth of individual human significance is that we should not grade people in importance. God makes all persons equally in his image, he is equally omniscient of all and responsive to all, and all stand equally immortal. In other words, as discussed earlier in this book, God is not a respecter of persons. Therefore, we also should treat and respect every person equally as a person.

Respect for persons may sometimes mean that we think more of a person than he does of himself. It also dictates that we have a high esteem and appreciation of ourselves, as we likewise are made in God's image and exhaustively known and regarded by him. Jesus says that the second great commandment is, "YOU SHALL LOVE YOUR NEIGHBOR AS YOURSELF" (Matthew 19:19). Here we are explicitly commanded to love ourselves as a prerequisite to loving our neighbors. One must have a proper understanding and appreciation of her own worth and dignity before she can have a proper regard for her neighbor. "To show partiality is not good," Solomon says (Proverbs 28:21).[1] New Testament writers agree.[2]

Jesus condemned the behavior of the Pharisees who loved respectful greetings that appeared to set them above others. He then added,

> But do not be called Rabbi; for One is your Teacher, and you are all brothers. And do not call anyone on earth your father; for One is your Father, He who is in heaven. And do not be called leaders; for One is your Leader, that is Christ. But the greatest among you shall be your servant. (Matthew 23:8-11)

Despite all of our pretentious titles, there is no superiority or inferiority of men. In *The Great Divorce*, C. S. Lewis says of the people in heaven, "They are all famous. They are all known, remembered, recognized by the only Mind that can give a perfect judgment."[3] There are no great men as compared with the rest of us, and there is no one "Man of the Year" or "Person of the Year," as *Time* would have us believe. A fanfare is a bright and brassy piece of music used to announce the appearance of royalty or other important people. In view of the significance of all persons before God, Aaron Copeland's "Fanfare for the Common Man" speaks a profound truth.

But that does not mean that human leadership—which ranks people in apparent importance—carries no validity. Human leadership serves as a necessary accommodation to a broken world. In a world without conflict, as before man's fall in Eden, there is no reason to set people over each other. Indeed, only after the fall did God make Adam the ruler of Eve (Genesis 3:16). This does not say that men command more significance than women or that other leaders enjoy greater significance than those they lead. It serves merely as a convenience or economy to control conflict among selfish, sinful people. That human leadership is a by-product of sin is clear from Scripture: "By the transgression of a land many are its princes" (Proverbs 28:2).

Proverbs speaks to the necessity of human leadership: "Where there is no guidance, the people fall, but in abundance of counselors there is victory" (Proverbs 11:14). There must be human leadership. Jesus fittingly called the leaderless multitudes "sheep without a shepherd" (Matthew 9:36). In other words, God has prescribed governments as an antidote to man's sinful tendencies. Paul concurs:

> Let every person be in subjection to the governing authorities. For there is no authority except from God, and those which exist are established by God. Therefore he who resists authority has opposed the ordinance of God; and they who have opposed will receive condemnation upon themselves. (Romans 13:1-2)

Men are not like the locusts that don't need leaders: "The locusts have no king, yet all of them go out in ranks" (Proverbs 30:27).

Scripture teaches that people who are leaders serve as God's regents on this rebellious planet. God is the one whom all people were made to follow, but, until he returns as king, people must act, although imperfectly, in his stead. The king's oath is before God (Ecclesiastes 8:2). Proverbs affirms, "A divine decision is in the lips of the king; his mouth should not err in judgment" (Proverbs 16:10).[4] Isaiah carries the truth further: "The LORD enters into judgment with the elders and princes of His people" (Isaiah 3:14).

Because human leaders act in place of God, he expects them to act righteously. Proverbs 16:12 says, "It is an abomination for kings to commit wickedness, for a throne is established on righteousness."[5] The responsibility of leaders to God is made clear by King Jehoshaphat's instructions to the judges he appointed:

> And he said to the judges, "Consider what you are doing, for you do not judge for man but for the LORD who is with you when you render judgment. Now then let the fear of the LORD be upon you; be very careful what you do; for the LORD our God will have no part in unrighteousness or partiality or the taking of a bribe." (2 Chronicles 19:6-7)

God's concern over the quality of human leadership is evident in Jesus' rebuke to the religious leaders of his day who misled the people:

> "But woe to you, scribes and Pharisees, hypocrites, because you shut off the kingdom of heaven from people; for you do not enter in yourselves, nor do you

allow those who are entering to go in. . . . Woe to you blind guides. . . . " (Matthew 23:13, 16)[6]

An enlightening example from Scripture of human leadership is Saul, Israel's first king. God considered Israel's demand for a human king as rejection of him (1 Samuel 8:4-22; 10:17-19; 2:12, 17-19). Nevertheless, God agreed to appoint a king. This king was Saul, a man who illustrates the problems of human leadership. Leaders are no less sinful than their subjects but often grow to think of themselves as more important and worthy than their subjects. Saul soon disobeyed God and was deposed by him (1 Samuel 15-16).

The Bible brims with other examples of human leadership. God chose many leaders: Joshua (Numbers 27:18; Deuteronomy 31:23; Joshua 1:1-2; 4:14), certain men to apportion the Promised Land (Numbers 34:16-29), David (1 Samuel 13:14; 2 Samuel 5:3-4, 12), the sons of Levi as priests (Deuteronomy 18:5; 21:5), Solomon (1 Chronicles 29:25), John the Baptist (Luke 1:5-17, 57), Jesus' apostles (Matthew 10:1-4), and Paul (Acts 9:1-17). Moreover, a coliseum of other examples of human leadership—including elders, prophets, and military commanders—crowd the Scriptures.[7]

Because God does approve of human leadership, we should respect and obey legitimate authority. As Proverbs says, "The wise of heart will receive commands" (Proverbs 10:8). The Scriptures clearly teach that we should obey our governments (Proverbs 24:21-22).[8] We should even rejoice that we have leaders. Nehemiah sets a precedent:

"Judah rejoiced over the priests and Levites who served" (Nehemiah 12:44).[9] Without human leaders, evil breeds even faster than at its usual frightening rate. The chaotic conditions in leaderless Israel are succinctly described in Judges: "In those days there was no king in Israel; everyone did what was right in his own eyes" (Judges 21:25). That effective human leadership serves as a blessing is also evident from Isaiah, in which God threatened to remove the leaders of Judah and Jerusalem as a punishment for sin (Isaiah 3:1-5).

So, human leadership stands as a valid and desirable thing, but whether one performs a leadership role is irrelevant to true significance. The peon is no less important than the president.

Questions for Reflection

1. If, as we saw in an earlier chapter, every person is equally significant before God, how should we treat people with regard to status, race, gender, and faults? How well do we do that?

2. In order to treat other persons with dignity, must a person first have a healthy respect for herself?

3. Do we rank persons in importance? Should we do so?

4. What does the Bible say about the validity of human leadership? What are some examples?

5. It seems necessary that we have human leaders, but how does that affect the significance of the leaders and the persons they lead?

6. According to Scripture, what should our attitude be toward persons who have legitimate authority over us?

15. Records Are Unessential

Whatever things were gain to me, those things I have counted as loss for the sake of Christ. . . . One thing I do: forgetting what lies behind and reaching forward to what lies ahead, I press on toward the goal for the prize of the upward call of God in Christ Jesus.
                                              —Philippians 3:7, 13-14

N either is it crucial to the significance of a person that he record and preserve his accomplishments, thoughts, words, deeds, and surroundings. As discussed in chapter 5, human efforts to do this really are futile.

First, a person stands poorly equipped to keep an adequate history of himself. Gaps lurk in our senses, just as they do between our fingers. Our eyes deliver limited resolving power, our ears hear only within a small frequency range, our noses apprehend only a few gases, our taste buds discern but few flavors, and our tactile sense cannot handle phenomena that are too small or large. And human spatial limitations severely restrict our ability accurately to observe and record happenings. One person is obviously inept to do so, but even all persons en masse compose such a small fraction of the whole universe that they are collectively unable merely to observe accurately a representative sample of aggregate reality.

But our spatial limits restrict us even more than this. We are peculiarly tied to our immediate surroundings. My little world—my job, house, family, friends, hometown—seems intrinsically more important than yours. It seems more important that the athletic teams from the city where I live do well than that those of other cities do well. It is revealing that the same house can be exciting and novel to new occupants, and yet boring and lifeless to previous occupants.

Our temporal finitude limits our ability not only to observe but also to record events. The average person lives on this planet a mere threescore years and ten (plus a few years nowadays), and humans as a species have kept records for some six thousand years at most. Again, the limitation squeezes more tightly than it appears. We are all peculiarly tied to our generations—our lifetimes. The events that we experience, and particularly those of the present, seem inherently more important than events that have occurred or will occur outside our lifetimes or the present moment. In short, we magnify and exaggerate the importance of the present.

In the autobiography of his early life, C. S. Lewis paints by metaphor a vivid picture of the narrow limits of our individual perspectives. He says that considering your "own happiness" as more important than "your neighbor's [is] like thinking that the nearest telegraph pole is really the largest."[1] We all fall into this trap. Almost automatically, it seems more important that I get a parking spot than the frustrated driver behind me, and that my child be admitted to a good college as opposed to the kids next door.

But our inability to observe and record all that occurs is not important inasmuch as the omniscient God maintains a complete and accurate history. Therefore, nothing is lost if I cannot remember something I did or a fire destroys my scrapbook. A past event is not less significant because the pictures I took didn't turn out, I failed to tape record it, or I forgot to get a souvenir. We don't have to seek frantically to capture every bit of beauty and perfection before it irretrievably disappears. Note that Jesus ignored Peter's offer at the transfiguration to preserve the occasion by building three tabernacles (Matthew 17:1-8).

So there is no intrinsic reason for one to keep a diary or scrapbook or trophy case. Christians especially should be sure that when they try to memorialize their thoughts in articles and books or their sounds and images on recordings, they are not merely seeking "to be noticed by men" (Matthew 23:5). I hope I am not doing that in the book you are now reading. Books and recordings should either say something different or repeat something that has already been said but to an audience not previously reached. If existing literature adequately covers a subject, the first impression must be that subsequent recitals are mere grasping for significance. This is not, however, an appeal for Christians to stop publishing and recording. If anything, we need more books and records, but our motives should be examined.

It is indeed good news that humans can safely forget the past. Ecclesiastes says that wisdom does not flow from comparing the past with the present: "Do not say, 'Why is it that the former days were better than these?' For it is not from wisdom that you ask about this" (Ecclesiastes 7:10). Jesus adds to this principle by dismissing the tradition of the elders that bound the Pharisees so tightly. He had no greater regard for an act because it was traditional. Paul even sets an example for intentionally forgetting the past, including his considerable accomplishments in Judaism. He says, "One thing I do: forgetting what lies behind and reaching forward to what lies ahead, I press on toward the goal for the prize of the upward call of God in Christ Jesus" (Philippians 3:13-14).

Compare Paul's perspective with the typical graduation ceremony or other transitional situation. People rush around shedding tears, taking pictures, getting addresses and autographs, and making recordings. The obvious fear is that whatever cannot be somehow humanly preserved will be lost forever. We act as if only that tiny portion of the present that we can push beyond the nonce with our cameras and recorders will stand as significant.

But if the omnipresent and eternal God knows everything that we do and acts in reference to all that we do, it is not a tragedy that a person forgets something. The true significance of the unidentified war casualties buried in mass graves around the world would not be increased if we knew each of their names and even life histories. The persons and events that human history misses are not rendered insignificant by the limitations of human knowledge. In other words, we do not save anything by erecting a monument to someone's memory or detailing his life in a biography.

Neither is it important that a person preserve her name by having children. A bachelor or childless woman stands equally significant as a person who has fifteen children. Also it is of no consequence to collect things or relics associated with the lives of noted people or with noted events. We don't owe it to the memory of George Washington to restore and preserve every tavern in which he slept. Isaiah said that when God devastated Damascus and cities of Aroer, men would not look to the things that they had made:

> In that day man will have regard for his Maker,
> And his eyes will look to the Holy One of Israel.
> He will not have regard for the altars, the work of his hands,
> Nor will he look to that which his fingers have made,
> Even the Asherim and incense stands. (Isaiah 17:7-8)

Instead, our significance flows from the character and attributes of God.

As they alone can be expected to appreciate this truth, Christians should examine their motives when recording events. We should be sure that we write church histories or biographies of ourselves or others for reasons other than the fallacy of ensuring our significance.

The Scriptures do not authorize humans to remember anything just to make history. Only commandments of God, acts of God, personal spiritual triumphs and lessons, and things that otherwise glorify God are approved by the Bible for memorialization. The Bible itself should be remembered, and Proverbs instructs us to remember God's commandments: "Bind them on your fingers; write them on the tablet of your heart" (Proverbs 7:3).[2] The psalmist testifies, "I will never forget Your precepts, for by them You have revived me" (Psalm 119:93).[3] Jesus encouraged his disciples by promising that the Holy Spirit would cause them to remember all that he said to them (John 14:26). And it is of paramount importance that Jesus' promise to rise from the dead was remembered by his followers after his crucifixion.

Moses encouraged Israel not to forget the law:

> Take to your heart all the words with which I am warning you today, which you shall command your sons to observe carefully, even all the words of this law. For it is not an idle word for you; indeed it is your life. And by this word you will prolong your days in the land, which you are about to cross the Jordan to possess. (Deuteronomy 32:46-47)

To ensure that Israel would remember the law, Moses "wrote this law and gave it to the priests, the sons of Levi who carried the ark of the covenant of the LORD, and to all the elders of Israel" (Deuteronomy 31:9). Moses coupled this act with a command to the

Levites that they read the law every seven years when Israel came together at the place that God would choose (Deuteronomy 31:10-13).[4]

Scripture also urges people to remember God's actions. Psalm 105:5 exhorts, "Remember His wonders which He has done, His marvels and the judgments uttered by His mouth."[5] Asaph says,

> I shall remember the deeds of the LORD;
> Surely I will remember Your wonders of old.
> I will meditate on all Your work
> And muse on Your deeds. (Psalm 77:11-12)

Moses commanded the people of Israel before they entered the Promised Land: "And you shall remember all the way which the LORD your God has led you in the wilderness these forty years" (Deuteronomy 8:2).[6] And David ordered his soul to "forget none of [God's] benefits" (Psalm 103:2).

The Bible also authorizes us to remember ours and others' spiritual victories. Moses remembered how God answered his prayers that rebellious Israel be spared (Deuteronomy 9:13-28). Caleb recalled that, as one of the spies who reconnoitered in the Promised Land when Israel first reached the banks of the Jordan forty-five years earlier, he "followed the LORD my God fully" and urged occupation of the land (Joshua 14:6-8). For purposes of instruction and encouragement we should record our spiritual journeys. Also, to the extent that we can learn from them, we should remember and write biographies of the lives of others. God comforted Joshua with reference to his dead predecessor: "Just as I have been with Moses, I will be with you; I will not fail you or forsake you" (Joshua 1:5). Jesus prepared his disciples for persecution by reminding them that the prophets before them also suffered persecution (Matthew 5:12). And the angel Gabriel promised Zacharias, the father of John the Baptist, that his son would come in the spirit and power of Elijah (Luke 1:16-17). In each of these instances, the lives of persons who had died were remembered and their memories had a beneficial effect.

A specific spiritual event that Jesus said would be remembered is the woman's anointing of his feet with the alabaster vial of costly perfume. Jesus said that "wherever this gospel is preached in the whole world, what this woman has done will also be spoken of in memory of her" (Matthew 26:6-7, 13; see also Mark 14:3, 9). Fittingly, we lack certainty of this woman's identity, but knowing her identity is not necessary to her deed being remembered as glorifying to God. And it is her deed that truly deserves to be remembered by other people. God knows her identity, and her significance stands secure through him— not through human memories.

To remind us of things that he has accomplished, God even approves of memorial ceremonies and monuments. Moses, for example, commanded Israel to remember God's deliverance from Egypt by celebrating the Passover (Deuteronomy 16:2-3). With the still-repeated words "do this in remembrance of Me," Jesus charged his disciples to commemorate his death (Luke 22:19-20).

The only monuments that God seems to approve in the Bible are those that serve to remind humans of what God has done. An illustration is God's commission of a monument to memorialize his miracle of parting the Jordan in order to permit Israel to cross into the Promised Land on dry ground. The twelve stones served as "a memorial to the sons of Israel forever" (Joshua 4:1-8).

Another instance is God's direction that a portion of manna be kept as a reminder of his provision. The book of Exodus tells us: "Then Moses said, 'This is what the LORD has commanded, "Let an omerful of it [manna] be kept throughout your generations, that they may see the bread that I fed you in the wilderness, when I brought you out of the land of Egypt" ' " (Exodus 16:32).[7]

Monuments to men are not generally approved by God. A case in point is when King Saul, who had strayed from obedience to God, set up a monument to himself at Mount Carmel after defeating the Amalekites (1 Samuel 15:12).

We need to remember parts of the past in order to learn and be encouraged, but not from fear that what we don't preserve stands lost forever. Another prevalent and similar attitude that clashes with the truth of every person's total significance is that our body of knowledge amounts to the only one in the universe and therefore every datum that can humanly be dug up must be squirreled away by us.

The fixation on human records may explain the sin of David's census. We are told: "Then Satan stood up against Israel and moved

185

David to number Israel" (1 Chronicles 21:1; 2 Samuel 24:1-10, 15). Apparently this census was sinful because it served no legitimate organizational purpose, as other censuses had, but was made for the sole purpose of finding out how many people made up the nation of Israel—perhaps for bragging rights. David commanded that the census be taken so "that I may know the number of the people." Modern instances of this abound: trying to discover the strongest man in the world, looking for the world's highest IQ, or seeking to discover what the neighbors are doing at this moment. The Psalms comfort by reminding us of God's omniscience: "The LORD will count when He registers the peoples" (Psalm 87:6).

It is appropriate to ask if we Christians should count the number of people who respond to our invitations to accept Christ or obsess over other measureable results of Christian endeavor. Conversion and church attendance statistics might well serve as a testimony to non-Christians or encouragement to believers, and, if so, decision cards should be collected, counted, and reported. But our motive should not be merely to collect facts and establish human records.

It is, moreover, often legitimate for Christians to inquire after what their neighbors are doing. Nehemiah, for example, who languished in captivity in Babylon, asked what was happening in Judah in order that he might pray and fast for the improvement of conditions there (Nehemiah 1:2-4). But this was done in order to advance God's kingdom, not merely to record human activity.

Questions for Reflection

1. What will happen if we don't keep a record of past events?

2. Are humans able to keep a complete and accurate record of all events? Why or why not?

3. Is it a tragedy if we don't recognize and preserve records of all human excellence? What is the basis for your answer?

4. What do you think C. S. Lewis meant when he said that considering your "own happiness" as more important than "your neighbor's [is] like thinking that the nearest telegraph pole is really the largest"? Is this a helpful insight?

5. Is there any inherently useful purpose in keeping a diary or scrapbook? What might that purpose be?

6. Why was Paul willing to forget his past accomplishments?

7. Would anything be added to the significance of the person buried in the Tomb of the Unknowns in Arlington Cemetery or to the significance of other persons buried anonymously in mass graves if we knew their identities? If so, what would that be?

8. In what circumstances does Scripture approve memorializing or recording events?

9. What are some examples of memorials approved by God? Why were these approved?

16. Free to Be Humble, Forgive, and Love Others

> *An argument started among [the disciples] as to which of them would be the greatest. But Jesus, knowing their thoughts, . . . said to them, "For it is the one who is least among all of you who is the greatest."*
>
> —Luke 9:46-48

The truth that every person stands securely significant as a result of God's omniscience and other teachings of Christianity frees us individually to be humble as God commands. Other people do not pose threats to our importance—we don't have to compete with them for God's attention. Therefore, one incurs no loss in deferring to others. I don't become less than you by letting you go first, admitting I'm wrong, or apologizing to you. And we should never be proud, because our significance depends entirely on something outside ourselves. Our importance does not consist in what we make of ourselves. So, there is no cause to be proud and no loss in being humble.

The Bible is replete with commands to be humble. "Let no one boast in men," Paul urges (1 Corinthians 3:21 NKJV). Proverbs 16:5 adds, "Everyone who is proud in heart is an abomination to the LORD; assuredly, he will not be unpunished." God is not pleased by human pride but rather by humility—"with the humble is wisdom" (Proverbs 11:2). We are exhorted by Scripture not to praise ourselves (Proverbs 27:2), not to "stand in the place of great men" (Proverbs 25:6-7), not to search out our own glory (Proverbs 25:27), not to take the places of honor at table (Luke 14:1, 7-11), and not to reveal all our knowledge (Proverbs 12:23).

Jesus has much to say about humility. He repeatedly told his disciples that the way to be great is to be the last in line, that is, to be a servant (Matthew 20:25-28; 23:5-12; Mark 9:33-35; Luke 22:24-27). At the Last Supper, after the disciples had again fought over "which one of them was regarded to be greatest" (Luke 22:24), Jesus taught the ultimate lesson of humility by washing the feet of his disciples, including the treacherous Judas (John 13:5-17). Indeed, Jesus taught that one cannot enter heaven unless he becomes humble like a child. Christian conversion is a most humbling thing in that it involves admitting one's sinfulness and casting one's self upon the mercy of God (Matthew 18:1-4).

God displays his approval of humility in the lives of many biblical characters. Numbers says of Moses, the only man with whom God spoke in a manner that could be called face to face: "Now the man Moses was very humble, more than any man who was on the face of the earth" (Numbers 12:3). Job said, "I do not take notice of myself" (Job 9:21). And the cry of John the Baptist can be heard: "After me comes

One who is mightier than I, and I am not even fit to stoop down and untie the thong of His sandals" (Mark 1:7).

But by far the most impressive biblical example of humility is the life of Jesus. He, the Lord of the universe, arrived in a stable and made his final entry in Jerusalem on the back of a borrowed donkey (Matthew 21:1-3, 6-9). He fraternized with social outcasts (Luke 7:34) and, as mentioned above, even washed the feet of his half-loyal disciples (John 13:3-17). As Jesus said, "I do not seek My glory" (John 8:50).[1]

A dramatic opposite of this example is this assertion by Adolf Hitler when it was suggested that he might be wrong: "I cannot be mistaken. What I do and say is historical."[2] That kind of insecure pride is completely inappropriate in view of the security of every person's significance in God's immutable character. We can afford to be humble, admit our mistakes, and submit to our parents and others in authority.

Not only does this truth of our significance permit us to be humble, but also it frees us to love one another. When we understand that our identity stands secure—that significance is not something to be wrested away from other people—we are enabled to love those other people. Others pose no threat to our importance. This truth of our individual significance puts us in a position to think and act beyond our interests. When you get sick, I can cry. "You shall love your neighbor as yourself," we are commanded (Leviticus 19:18; Matthew 19:19; Romans 13:9). Not only are we to love each other as ourselves, but also we should "regard one another as more important than [ourselves]"

193

(Philippians 2:3-4).[3] The command does not tell us to that others are actually better than we are, but rather that we are to "regard" them as better. This is *agape* or supernatural love that exists between even very few spouses. Only in awareness of the truth of individual human significance can one consistently act in such disregard of one's self.

Paul, who knew that his identity was safe, repeatedly urges that Christians arrange their behavior with reference to others. "Rejoice with those who rejoice, and weep with those who weep," he urges (Romans 12:15). In other words, love requires one not to be joyful while his neighbor is hurting, and yet to forget his troubles and rejoice with his neighbor when the neighbor is happy. Paul explains, "I also please all men in all things, not seeking my own profit but the profit of the many, that they may be saved" (1 Corinthians 10:32-33).

Christians are even exhorted to give up things that are legitimate and good for the sake of not offending others. "Therefore, if food causes my brother to stumble, I will never eat meat again, that I might not cause my brother to stumble," Paul says (1 Corinthians 8:13).[4] In fact, Paul felt so deeply for others that he mourned over sin that did not belong to him (1 Corinthians 5:1-2; 2 Corinthians 11:29; 12:21). Ezra was sufficiently exercised about the sin of other people of Judah that he, while in Babylon, tore his garment, pulled out some of his hair, and fell down before God in prayer (Ezra 9:1-6).

Self-interest or the profit motive did not govern in Jesus' dealings with others. On one occasion, in order to minister to the needs of a multitude of more than five thousand persons, Jesus interrupted the solitude to which he had withdrawn upon hearing of John the Baptist's execution (Matthew 14:10-23).[5] Indeed, Jesus' entire mission to this earth was of ultimate self-denial and altruism (Romans 15:3; Philippians 2:5-8).

Recall the earlier discussion of how some philanthropists give in order to attract attention. The Pharisees of Jesus' day engaged in this practice (Matthew 6:2-4). But the truths of Christianity render it pointless because God, upon whom our significance depends, knows our every move anyway. Ironically, ancient Jewish wisdom as expressed in the Talmud, which the Pharisees apparently did not follow very well, advised that in the highest forms of charity the giver's identity remains hidden from the beneficiary.[6] This is, for example, what ordinarily occurs when one nowadays donates blood through the International Red Cross: The donor never knows who will receive her blood or even if it will be used at all.

Consider the selflessness of Jonathan's love for David. As the son of King Saul, Jonathan stood in line to assume his father's throne. By all human motives, he should have opposed and even hated David, who contended for his father's throne (1 Samuel 20:31-32). Yet Jonathan dared to love David "as . . . his own life." He even gave David his robe, armor, and sword (1 Samuel 18:1, 3-4; 20:17). When Saul decided to kill David, Jonathan fasted and grieved. Jonathan's supernatural love for David is best summarized by this open-ended offer to David: "Whatever you say, I will do for you" (1 Samuel 20:4).

But it's not enough just to return the love of those who love us. Scripture commands us to love our enemies. Jesus instructed his disciples: "Treat others the same way you want them to treat you. If you love those who love you, what credit is that to you? For even sinners love those who love them. If you do good to those who do good to you, what credit is that to you? For even sinners do the same" (Luke 6:31-33).[7]

Paul adds, "Bless those who persecute you; bless and curse not" (Romans 12:14). Biblical standards direct us even to feed our enemy when he is hungry and give him drink when he is thirsty (Proverbs 25:21-22; Romans 12:17-21). And Jesus teaches that the duty of Christians is to be reconciled to those who have grudges against them, regardless of who bears the fault (Matthew 5:23-24).

The scriptural examples of loving one's enemies set a rigorous precedent. David spared the life of Saul although he could have easily killed him, and when Saul died David chanted a lament (1 Samuel 24:1-22; 2 Samuel 1:17-27). Elisha once spared and fed the Syrians who sought his life (2 Kings 6:21-23). And on the cross Jesus cried on behalf of his merciless killers: "Father, forgive them; for they do not know what they are doing" (Luke 23:34).

A modern-day instance of loving one's enemies is furnished by the life of Richard Wurmbrand. A Romanian pastor, Wurmbrand endured fourteen years in communist prisons. As his last act in Romania before leaving for the West, he placed a flower on the grave of the colonel who had given the order for his arrest.[8]

Narcissism, or self-absorption, has always been a temptation for humans. Its incidence seems, however, to have increased in Western society beginning in the 1970s with the advent of celebrity magazines, followed by reality television shows, and then the Internet (complete with social media websites).[9] But there is no reason to be narcissistic inasmuch as an individual's significance stands secure and does not depend on the attention he receives from other people.

Nothing you could do to me can threaten my significance. Therefore, I have no grounds to be indignant at any insult or slander you may cast at me. It makes sense to "turn the other cheek" when slapped across the face with an insult. I am not reduced by backing down to someone or by refusing to respond to calumny. Paul says, "For you bear with anyone if . . . he hits you in the face" (2 Corinthians 11:20). The only thing that the Scripture authorizes the Christian to be indignant at are sins against God and other people.

Another part of the Christian's love for others should be the surrender of legitimate rights. The Bible affords no precedent for demanding equal rights for oneself. Jesus taught that a worker should not grumble because another gets paid the same for less work (Matthew 20:1-16).[10] On another occasion Jesus refused to tell a man's brother to divide the family inheritance (Luke 12:13-15). Also,

197

Scripture requires the Christian to pay his own debts, and yet forgive the debts of others. One has a legal right to repayment of a loan, but we are commanded to give to whoever asks of us and demand no repayment. Jesus teaches his disciples:

> If you lend to those from whom you expect to receive, what credit is that to you? Even sinners lend to sinners in order to receive back the same amount. But love your enemies, and do good, and lend, expecting nothing in return; and your reward will be great, and you will be sons of the Most High; for He Himself is kind to ungrateful and evil men. (Luke 6:34-35)[11]

Again, consider 2 Corinthians 11:20, where Paul says: "For you tolerate it if anyone . . . devours you, anyone takes advantage of you." The Christian is even directed to forgo just lawsuits against his fellow believers (1 Corinthians 6:1-8). The rationale of this surrender of rights lies in the individual person's inherent significance (due to the character and acts of God), which makes recognition of her rights by other human beings unnecessary.

Forgiveness of others is a related ingredient in our love for others. As God forgives us, so should we forgive. To forgive those who have wronged us constitutes palpable evidence of the invisible God. Proverbs 19:11 says that "it is [a man's] glory to overlook a transgression." Paul affirms, "Love. . . does not take into account a wrong suffered" (1 Corinthians 13:4-5)[12] and urges all to "be kind to one another, tender-hearted, forgiving each other, just as God in Christ also has forgiven you" (Ephesians 4:32). Jesus commands Peter to forgive "up to seventy times seven" his brother who sins against him (Matthew 18:21-22). And Jesus extends the truth to say that one who does not forgive men will not be forgiven by God (Matthew 6:14-15). But Jesus' most eloquent teaching regarding this subject is his dying plea: "Father, forgive them" (Luke 23:34). It is also compelling that, while being unjustly stoned, Stephen prayed these shocking words before he died: "Lord, do not hold this sin against them!" (Acts 7:60). Unless one stands sure of his identity and significance, he cannot possibly forgive wrongs that jeopardize his earthly status. If worldly fame forms the extent of a person's significance, it is a heinous and unforgiveable crime to deprive a person of the opportunity to become famous or leave a legacy.

A somewhat surprising consequence of individual human significance is that even one's evil deeds cannot be ignored. The state should, as God's regent, punish the wicked deeds of people, leaving intact the commandment to individuals to ignore and forgive evil committed against them personally. A view that often prevails today is that no punishment is just unless it rehabilitates the one punished and/or deters him or others from committing the same crime again. This idea can even be traced back to Socrates, who says, "Now the proper office of punishment is two: he who is rightly punished ought either to become better and profit by it, or he ought to be made an example to his fellows, that they may see what he suffers, and fear and become better."[13] The Bible describes deterrence as a consideration in God's commandment that the state punish wrongdoers (Deuteronomy 13:11; 17:13; 19:20; 21:21).

Beyond deterrence, punishment serves a necessary corollary of two truths: the absolute nature of God's laws and the significance of individual humans. So, we should punish out of respect for man's significance. This is the real basis of penology. When the state refuses to punish what God has forbidden, it treats people as nothing. Which is more unkind, to punish a person or treat him as if he does not exist?

The reality of individual human significance can be seen in the general rule of punishment with which God charges the state. Exodus 21:23-25 presents the rule of *lex talionis*: "But if there is any further injury, then you shall appoint as a penalty life for life, eye for eye, tooth for tooth, hand for hand, foot for foot, burn for burn, wound for wound, bruise for bruise." Injuries to people are important only if people have value.

As we have seen, because our individual significance is secure, we can all venture to forgive and be humble. But this doesn't mean that evil deeds should be without consequences.

Questions for Reflection

1. Can anything happen that would change the fact that you are made in God's image, known to God, interacted with by God, and immortal? If so, what might that be?

2. In view of the completeness of individual human significance under the teachings of Christianity, can you afford to turn the other cheek? Can you afford to surrender your legitimate rights? Why or why not?

3. Is the significance of a person reduced by admitting that he is wrong, apologizing, or letting others go first? Explain your answer.

4. In his teachings, how did Jesus encourage humility? What example did he set in his life?

5. What are some biblical examples of humility?

6. Although mistreatment does not threaten one's individual significance, should the wrongful acts of others be ignored? Would ignoring the wrongful acts of a person be treating him with respect? Why or why not?

17. Free to Enjoy the Purpose of Life

> *But I do not consider my life of any account as dear to myself, in order that I may finish my course, and the ministry which I received from the Lord Jesus, to testify solemnly of the gospel of the grace of God.*
>
> —Acts 20:24

> *I want to leave a legacy*
> *How will they remember me?*
> *Did I choose to love?*
> *Did I point to You enough*
> *To make a mark on things*
> *I want to leave an offering*
> *A child of mercy and grace*
> *Who blessed Your name unapologetically*
> *And leave that kind of legacy*
> — Nichole Nordeman, "I Want to Leave a Legacy"

A final consequence of the truth of individual human significance is that each of us stands free to follow the purpose for which we were created, to live in reference to God. Despite our wistful mottoes and sayings about the luster and nobility of each person seeking his own niche and marching to the beat of his own private drummer, only God is our portion. Poet William Henley's defiant concluding words in "Invictus"—"I am the master of my fate: I am the captain of my soul"—ring hollow.

We are not masters of anything, and our faces do not shine with purpose until bowed low before Almighty God. Our purpose remains singular: "Let everything that has breath praise the LORD" (Psalm 150:6). The Westminster Shorter Catechism declares, "Man's chief end is to glorify God and to enjoy Him forever."[1] Indeed, "life" is defined in such terms by Scripture: "For with You is the fountain of life; in Your light we see light," David says (Psalm 36:9). Jesus says to know God "is eternal life" (John 17:3) and that belief in him even yields life "abundantly" (John 10:10). And Paul concurs: "Christ . . . is our life" (Colossians 3:4).[2]

Because the omnipotent, omnipresent, and eternal God has made us in his image, counts our days and steps and even hairs, responds to us, and has made us live forever, we don't have to establish our identity. We need not seek our own but can comfortably live to please God. Forgetting ourselves, we can move closer to the numerous biblical commandments regarding our purpose. The greatest commandment is, "YOU SHALL LOVE THE LORD YOUR GOD WITH ALL YOUR HEART, AND WITH ALL YOUR SOUL, AND WITH ALL YOUR MIND" (Matthew 22:37-40; Deuteronomy 11:1). Jesus also said that "whoever loses his life for My sake shall find it" and that one should "take up his cross and follow Me" (Matthew 16:24-25).[3]

Knowing that our significance is secure, we can lose our lives for Christ—we can "decrease" before him, as John the Baptist said (John 3:25-30). Paul makes frequent reference to what our purpose should be. He determined to "know nothing among you except Jesus

Christ, and Him crucified" (1 Corinthians 2:2). Paul considered his life of no account that he might complete the ministry given him by God (Acts 20:24). His ambition, he said, was "whether at home or absent, to be pleasing to Him" (2 Corinthians 5:9). "Whether, then, you eat or drink or whatever you do, do all to the glory of God," Paul exhorts (1 Corinthians 10:31).[4] For the sake of Christ and God's kingdom, Paul was even willing to be a "spectacle to the world," a fool "for Christ's sake," "weak," "without honor," "hungry and thirsty," "poorly clothed," "roughly treated," "homeless," "reviled," "persecuted," and "slandered." He summarized that he and the other apostles had been treated as "the scum of the world, the dregs of all things" (1 Corinthians 4:9-13). Most of us are far too in love with apparent prestige to accept this treatment.

We are told that we should sell all that we have for the kingdom of heaven (Matthew 13:44-46). Jesus' disciples practiced this principle: Many of them left everything, including their jobs, families, and homes, in order to follow Jesus (Matthew 4:18-22; Luke 5:27-28). As Jesus told Martha, "only one thing is necessary"—sitting at the feet of Jesus (Luke 10:38-42). Popularity is not necessary. The apostles were "without honor" (1 Corinthians 4:9-10), and Jesus disdained public approval (Matthew 15:1-2, 10-13). Indeed, Jesus rebuked the scribes and Pharisees who lived for human approval (Matthew 6:1-6; 23:5). Neither does purpose flow from material possessions. "For what will it profit a man if he gains the whole world and forfeits his soul? Or what will a man give in exchange for his soul?" Jesus asks (Matthew 16:26). Recall that the decision of the rich young man who refused to give his possessions to the poor left him "grieving" (Matthew 19:16, 21-22). Jesus teaches us that heaven, not earth, constitutes the only safe place to invest one's treasure (Matthew 6:19-21).

All of our lives' activities down to the smallest minutiae should be marshaled in service to God. Eating and drinking (1 Corinthians 10:31),[5] our thoughts (2 Corinthians 10:5), the decision to marry or remain single (Matthew 19:12; 22:23-30; 1 Corinthians 7:29-35), one's children (1 Samuel 1:21-28; Luke 1:26-35, 38, 57-63), charity (Mark 14:3-8), and one's relationship with his family (Matthew 8:21-22; 10:34-37; 19:29) should be dedicated to pleasing only God.

Even one's death should be calculated to glorify God. Jesus rebuked Peter for ignoring God's interests by suggesting that Jesus not suffer and die (Matthew 16:21-23). Samson in his death killed more wicked Philistines than in his life. In his blindness, he prayed that God would strengthen him "just this time," and he brought down on himself and the enemies of the kingdom the building that was his prison (Judges 16:25-30). And Paul was ready to die or live for the sake of Christ. His interest was that "Christ shall even now, as always, be exalted in [his] body, whether by life or by death" (Philippians 1:20-26).[6] Recall that Paul willingly sacrificed all of the "accomplishments" of his former life for the sake of Christ (Philippians 3:4-8). In short, our lives should be poured out before God like the alabaster vial of costly perfume used to anoint Jesus (Matthew 26:6-13).[7]

We should even take our identity from Christ. In other words, we should define ourselves in relation to him. When the Jews who had renewed construction of the temple in defiance of Artaxerxes were asked their names by Persian officials, they answered, "We are the servants of the God of heaven and earth" (Ezra 5:10-11). When John the Baptist was asked who he was, he would answer only, "I am a VOICE OF ONE CRYING IN THE WILDERNESS, 'MAKE STRAIGHT THE WAY OF THE LORD,' as Isaiah the prophet said" (John 1:19-23). Paul's favorite titles for himself were "an apostle of Jesus Christ" and "a bondservant of Christ." Considering his accomplishments (i.e., his human legacy) to be "loss" and even "rubbish so that [he might] gain Christ" (Philippians 3:8), Paul said that he was "crucified" or dead and it was Christ who lived in him (Galatians 2:20).

The analogy of the Christian's relationship to Christ as marriage adds to this truth. Scripture compares Jesus with the bridegroom and believers with his bride (Matthew 9:14-15; 25:1-13; John 3:29; 2 Corinthians 11:2). Just as the bride historically sacrificed her former identity and was happy to be known only as the wife of her husband, so we as Christians should be content to be known by the name of Christ, that is, as Christians. And the fact that God has made each of us in his image, knows each of us exhaustively, acts in response to each of us, and causes each of us to live forever, permits us to lose our lives in the purpose of pleasing him. It is not necessary that we leave memories and mementoes here on earth. We can afford, as Charles Swindoll puts it, to be "willing unknowns" in the service of the King.[8] Oswald Chambers writes that through "the supernatural grace of God" we can "live twenty-four hours in every day as a saint, . . . go through drudgery as a disciple, . . . live an ordinary, unobserved, ignored existence as a disciple of Jesus." He continues, "It is inbred in us that we have to do exceptional things for God; but we have not. We have to be exceptional in the ordinary things, to be holy in mean streets, among mean people."[9] The doctrines of Christianity teach us that, with respect to individual humans, there is no oblivion.

None of us practices these principles very well, and implementing them is never a battle that is won. On one particular day, I may confidently devote myself to the purpose of glorifying God, secure in my significance based on the truths of Christianity. But I may lose the battle the next day—finding myself, for example, offering my prayers and charitable donations for approving feedback from other people instead of directing them to God, the Audience of One. Recall that it was not just the scribes and Pharisees who did "all their deeds to be noticed by men" (Matthew 23:2-5). The disciples also debated "which of them was the greatest" (Mark 9:31-34).

We believe that the Christian doctrines establishing individual human significance stand true not because we perceive that they are so. Rather, we believe them by faith. After all, "we walk by faith, not by sight" (2 Corinthians 5:7).[10] And, in ways we do not understand, we are "blessed" because we do "not see, and yet believe[]" (John 20:29).[11] Of course, believing on the basis of faith does not make a belief unreasonable. One may have good reasons and evidence for believing what one cannot perceive. Although we cannot presently perceive that they are true, we believe in subatomic physics, electromagnetic radiation, history (the consensus view of past events), and many other things we do not perceive. We believe these things on the basis of considerable evidence and good arguments. The teachings of Christianity are also supported by considerable evidence and good arguments. These arguments are what Paul used to persuade hearers on his missionary journeys to become believers.[12]

It comes down to the same question asked by the doubt-filled children of Israel during their wanderings in the desert: "Is the LORD among us, or not?" (Exodus 17:7). By faith, I believe he is among us and each of us is therefore fully significant.

Because they can fly, birds have no fear of heights. Because fish are as at home in the ocean as we humans are on land, they have no fear of water just as we have no fear of land. Inasmuch as our individual significance is secure, we likewise can traverse the often drudgery-filled days of our lives with no fear of oblivion. Regardless of how obscure we feel, none of us is a loser, wimp, or even a mere mortal. C. S. Lewis captured this truth: "There are no ordinary people.

You have never talked to a mere mortal."[13] This means that your family members who died young and mine too (including my father and first wife) are fully significant, no less than the most famous among us.

Questions for Reflection

1. According to the teachings of Scripture, what is the purpose of every human life?

2. How does devoting yourself to service of God, as opposed to promoting yourself, affect your opportunities for significance?

3. Is it true, as it appears on the surface, that in order to secure your significance you must make an individual mark or leave a legacy on the world? Why or why not?

4. How do John the Baptist and Paul illustrate abandonment of self-interest in favor of service to God?

5. How do the Christian teachings of the *imago dei*, God's omniscience of the details of every person's life, God's interaction with individual persons, and human immortality make it unnecessary to seek to be noticed and remembered by other persons?

6. Under the teachings of Christianity, can even the person who is most unnoticed and unaccomplished be dismissed as a loser, wimp, or geek? How do you explain your answer?

7. What does C. S. Lewis say about the value of every person? Do you agree or disagree, and why?

Endnotes

Preface

1. Michael Farquhar, *A Treasury of Foolishly Forgotten Americans* (New York: Penguin, 2008), 42, 44-45.
2. "Assassin's Diary," *Harper's Magazine* (January 1973), 62.
3. G. I. Williamson, *The Westminster Shorter Catechism: For Study Classes* (Phillipsburg, NJ: P&R Publishing, 1970 [1643-1652]), 1.

Chapter 1, Unhappily Insignificant

1. Nikos Kazantzakis, *Zorba the Greek* (New York: Simon & Schuster, 1952), 270.
2. Bede, *Ecclesiastical History of the English People*, chap. 13 (London: Penguin, 1955 [731]), 129-30.
3. John M. Barry, *The Great Influenza* (New York: Penguin Group, 2004), 306.
4. Os Guinness, *The Call* (Nashville: Thomas Nelson, 2003), 18.
5. Robert Descharnes and Gilles Neret, *Salvador Dali* (Cologne: Taschen, 1998); Christopher Smith, "Full-of-Themselves Famous People," http://www.cnn.com/2007/LIVING/worklife /09/28/mf.prima.donnas/ (accessed September 18, 2009).

6. Dotson Rader, "My Life Changed Forever," *Parade* (October 5, 2003), 5.

7. People, *Time* (November 20, 1972), 50.

8. Leo Braudy, *The Frenzy of Renown* (New York: Vintage, 1997), 424, 425, 464.

Chapter 2, Efforts at Significance, Part One

1. Leo Braudy, *The Frenzy of Renown* (New York: Vintage, 1997), 378-79, 386, 488, 570.

2. Miguel de Unamuno, *Tragic Sense of Life*, trans. J. E. Crawford Flitch (New York: Dover Publications, 2011 [1912]), 34.

3. J. Christopher Herold, ed. and trans., *The Mind of Napoleon* (New York: Columbia University Press, 1955), 39-40.

4. Ibid., 50.

5. Braudy, *Frenzy of Renown*, 75-76 n. 1.

6. Hannah Arendt, *The Human Condition* (Chicago: University of Chicago Press, 1958), 95.

7. Unamuno, *Tragic Sense of Life*, 166 n. 2.

8. William Law, *A Serious Call to a Devout and Holy Life* (London: Printed for William Innys, 1732), 237.

9. Stephen Moss, "Wit, Wisdom, and Not a Burgundy Tie in Sight," *The Guardian* (April 10, 2002), http://www.guardian.

co.uk/media/2002/apr/10/broadcasting.queenmother (accessed September 25, 2009).

10. http://www.theroyalforums.com/4778-4778/ (accessed March 21, 2013).

11. http://www.factmonster.com/spot/royal2.html (accessed September 26, 2009); http://www. prestigetitles.com/ (accessed September 26, 2009).

12. http://www.regaltitles.com/ (accessed September 26, 2009).

13. Clive Chessman and Jonathan Williams, *Rebels, Pretenders, and Imposters* (London: The British Museum Press, 2000), 12.

14. Ibid., 125.

15. Ibid., 125-31.

16. Ibid., 132-38.

17. Ibid., 130.

18. Ibid., 132. According to Chessman and Williams, "Both reigning and aspirant dynasties [have] indulged widely in historical fictions to embroider the fame of their past and present members. No royal family has been royal forever; all arrived at their sovereign position either through war or marriage." Ibid., 9.

19. *Almanac and Book of Facts* (1973).

20. Tyler Cowen, *What Price Fame?* (Cambridge, MA: Harvard University Press, 2000), 7. See also http://www.answers.com/topic/list-of-halls-and-walks-of-fame (accessed May 25, 2007), which lists dozens of halls of fame, including the Canadian Rodeo

Hall of Fame and the Robot Hall of Fame. At Warm Springs, Georgia, there is a Polio Hall of Fame. There are even affordable housing halls of fame—see Bryan M. Cavan, "Hall of Fame to Induct Renée Glover," *The Fulton County Daily Report* (October 13, 2009), http://bipartisanpolicy.org/about/housing-commission-members/ren%C3%A9e-lewis-glover (accessed December 8, 2013). This hall is not to be confused with the West Virginia Affordable Housing Hall of Fame: http://www.habitatwv.org/WVAHHOF/ (accessed October 14, 2009).

21. http://en.wikipedia.org/wiki/Honor_society, listing more than two hundred honor societies (accessed April 18, 2011).

22. David J. Miller and Michel Hersen, eds., *Research Fraud in the Behavioral and Biomedical Sciences* (New York: John Wiley & Sons, 1992), 9, quoting R. K. Merton, "Behavior Patterns of Scientists," *American Scientist* 57 (1969), 7. See also Cowen, *What Price Fame?* 1; Hal Hellman, *Great Feuds in Medicine* (New York: John Wiley & Sons, 2001), xi-xii, discussing "priority disputes in medical science" such as those "among Morton, Wells, and Jackson in the development of a useful anesthetic; between Banting and Macleod in the discovery of insulin; between Gujillemin and Schally in the discovery of the brain hormone; and between Gallo and Montagnier in the discovery of the Aids virus"; Hal Hellman, *Great Feuds in Science* (New York: John Wiley & Sons, 1998), xii; Ira Flatow, *They All Laughed* (New York: Harper

Collins, 1993), xii: "inventors had epic fights over the right to be called 'first' with an idea."

23. H. D. Anthony, *Sir Isaac Newton* (New York: Abelard Schuman, 1960), 65-72.

24. David Callahan, *The Cheating Culture* (New York: Harcourt, 2004), 9-10, 220-24.

25. 18 U.S.C. § 704(b). The U.S. Supreme Court has now declared the law unconstitutional as an infringement of free speech. *United States v. Alvarez*, 132 S.Ct. 2537 (2012). See John Crewdson, "Fake Claims of War Heroics a Federal Offense," *Chicago Tribune* (May 27, 2008), http://www.chicagotribune.com/news/nationworld/chi-valormay28,0,4768252.story (accessed November 7, 2010).

26. Michael Farquhar, *A Treasury of Foolishly Forgotten Americans* (New York: Penguin, 2008), 42.

27. Ibid., 44-45.

28. William Johnson, "The World's Greatest," *Sports Illustrated* (April 8, 1974), 102-12.

29. Norris McWhirter and Ross McWhirter, *Guinness Book of World Records* (New York: Sterling Publishing, 2011), http://www.guinnessworldrecords.com/ (accessed August 26, 2009). "Since first receiving a skin piercing in January 1997, Elaine Davidson (Brazil/UK) has been pierced a total of 4,225 times as of 8 June 2006." http://www.guinnessworldrecords.com/world-records/1/mostpiercings-in-a-lifetime-female) (accessed August 7, 2013).

More recently, forty-two-year-old Donna Simpson, a New Jersey mother who weighs 602 pounds, said she is determined to gain weight until she tips the scales at 1,000 pounds. Even before reaching this goal, she has made a submission to *Guinness* requesting that she be "named biggest to give birth and heaviest living woman." David K. Li, "NJ Woman Attempting to Become World's Fattest Lady," *New York Post* (March 15, 2010), http://www.nypost.com/p/news/local/nj_woman_attempting_to_become_world_pco3O4qPWiCg3yjE Waxx9N (accessed April 8, 2010).

30. "He Swims from Alcatraz as Preparation for Stunt," *The Atlanta Constitution* (December 11, 1972), 6-A.

31. Russell Baker, "Observer; The Demon Success," *The New York Times* (April 20, 1996), http://www.nytimes.com/1996/04/20/opinion/observer-the-demon-success.html?ref=jessicadubroff (accessed May 26, 2012).

32. Andrew Evans and Glenn D. Wilson, *Fame: The Psychology of Stardom* (London: Vision Paperbacks, 1999), 4.

33. www.nameastarlive.com (accessed July 16, 2009); www.nameastar.net (accessed July 16, 2009); www.starregistry.com (accessed July 16, 2009); www.intlstarregistry.com (accessed July 16, 2009).

34. www.nameastarlive.com (accessed July 16, 2009).

35. The website of the International Astronomical Union warns against these services: http://www.iau.org/public_press/themes/buying_

star_names/ (accessed July 17, 2009) ("Some commercial enterprises purport to offer such services for a fee. However, such 'names' have no formal or official validity whatever.").

36. "Leave a Legacy Application Agreement," distributed by Walt Disney World Company, undated.

37. Eric Berne, *Games People Play* (New York: Grove Press, 1964), 166.

38. Robert Frank, *Richistan* (New York: Crown Publishers, 2007), 97-102, 119.

39. H. Sidey, "Outracing the Past," *Time* (January 29, 1973), 15.

40. Charles Hellinger, "Farmer Built Statue to Self," *The Atlanta Constitution* (April 13, 1975), 2-D.

41. Gwendolyn Brooks, "Boy Breaking Glass," in *Blacks* (Chicago: Third World Press, 1987).

42. http://www.absoluteastronomy.com/topics/Eponym (accessed August 15, 2009); http:// www.alphadictionary.com/articles/eponyms/index.html (accessed August 15, 2009); http:// whonamedit.com/ (accessed August 15, 2009); Eugene Garfield, "What's in a Name? The Eponymic Route to Immortality," in *Essays of an Information Scientist* (Philadelphia: ISI Press, 1984), 384-95, http://www. garfield.library.upenn.edu/essays/v6p384y1983.pdf (accessed August 15, 2009); D. W. G. Ballentyne and D. R. Lovett, *A Dictionary of Named Effects and Laws in Chemistry, Physics, and Mathematics* (New York: Chapman & Hall, 1980); R. K. Merton, "Priorities in Scientific Discovery," in *The Sociology of Science:*

Theoretical and Empirical Investigations (Chicago: University of Chicago Press, 1973), 286-324.

43. It is particularly common for places to be named for politicians, often while they are still living. John Stossel and Myrna Toledo, "What's in a Building's Name? A Lot of Tax Dollars" (March 21, 2007), http://abcnews.go.com/2020/story?id=2967219&page=1#. UUtifleyLtw (accessed March 21, 2013). In West Virginia, "more than 30 buildings, a bridge and even a telescope" were named for Senator Robert Byrd while he was still living. Ibid.

44. For example, Alexander the Great founded eighteen cities that were named for him. Braudy, *Frenzy of Renown*, 36.

45. According to http://whonamedit.com/ (accessed August 5, 2009), in medicine alone there are more than fifteen thousand eponymous terms. See Barry G. Firkin and J. A. Whitworth, *Dictionary of Medical Eponyms*, 2nd ed. (New York: Informa HealthCare, 2001).

46. An *Aktion Reinhard* was the Nazi practice of genocidal killing of Jews in an area of Poland. It was named for Reinhard Heydrich. As one scholar says, "In the value-inverted world of Germany during the Nazi period, naming a genocidal undertaking after someone— in this case, the assassinated Reinhard Heydrich—was to honor him." This scholar says that between March 1942 and November 1943, the Germans used this method to kill "around two million Polish Jews." Daniel Jonah Goldhagen, *Hitler's Willing Executioners* (New York: Vintage, 1997), 196, and nn. 55, 56.

47. Stanley Jablonski, *Jablonski's Dictionary of Syndromes and Eponymic Diseases*, 2nd ed. (Malabar, FL: Krieger Publishing, 1991); James Pearre, "What a Way to Achieve Immortality," *Chicago Tribune* (March 19, 1976), 1, 4 (discussing eponymous disease names).

48. Garfield, "What's in a Name?" 384-95, available at http://www.garfield.library.upenn.edu/essays/v6p384y1983.pdf (accessed August 15, 2009), citing a source that lists twenty thousand eponyms.

49. Robert Lenzner, *The Great Getty* (New York: New American Library, 1985), 6.

50. Charles Elliott, *"Mr. Anonymous": Robert W. Woodruff of Coca-Cola* (Atlanta: Cherokee Publishing, 1982), 60.

51. Ibid., 270, 291.

52. Ibid., 60-61, 81, 149, 153, 170-71, 194, 258-59, 267.

53. Ron Alsop, "B-School Naming Rights: A Peek at the Price Tag," *College Journal* (from *The Wall Street Journal*) (September 20, 2004).

54. Ibid.

55. Elizabeth Bernstein, "The Higher Cost of Giving: Colleges Raise Bar for Donors," *The Wall Street Journal* (July 7, 2005). See also Keith Matheny, "Building-Naming Policies Being Reshaped by Controversies," *USA Today* (March 12, 2012), 2A.

56. Alsop, "B-School Naming Rights."

57. Ibid.

58. http://www.atlanta-airport.com/Airport/ATL/Airport_History.aspx (accessed August 7, 2013); "Hartsfield Family Speaks Out on Renaming Atlanta Airport," *USA Today* (September 23, 2003), http://www.usatoday.com/travel/news/2003/09/23-atl-name.htm (accessed March 18, 2010).

59. Jib Fowles, *Starstruck* (Washington, D.C.: Smithsonian Institution, 1992), 255.

60. Bernard Le Bovier de Fontenelle, *Nouveaux Dialogues des Morts*, ed. Donald Schier (Chapel Hill: University of North Carolina Press, 1965 [1683]), 108-11.

61. Fowles, *Starstruck*, 179.

62. Ed Grisamore, "Elvis Odd Spot," *Macon Telegraph* (August 15, 2004).

63. Jake Halpern, *Fame Junkies* (New York: Houghton Mifflin, 2007), 159-184; Fowles, *Starstruck*, 182-183.

64. Fowles, *Starstruck*, 175.

65. Halpern, *Fame Junkies*, 112-116; Fowles, *Starstruck*, ix, 7-8, 22-39, 63-78, 170-171, 191.

66. Halpern, *Fame Junkies*, 126-128, 194-195; Cooper Lawrence, *The Cult of Celebrity* (Guilford, Conn.; Globe Pequot Press, 2009), 32-33.

67. Halpern, *Fame Junkies*, 81, 84; http://www.acpa-la.com/ (accessed May 2, 2013).

68. http://en.wikipedia.org/wiki/Zapruder_film (accessed February 22, 2010).

69. Cowen, *What Price Fame?* 88.

70. Fowles, *Starstruck*, 247-248.

71. http://www.eimpersonators.com/impersonators_listings.html (accessed May 7, 2010).

72. http://apepta.webs.com/codeofconduct.htm (accessed May 7, 2010).

73. Andrew Ferguson, *Land of Lincoln* (New York: Grove Press, 2007), 153.

74. http://www.gigmasters.com/Impersonators/ (accessed February 8, 2010).

75. Tom Payne, *Fame* (New York: Picador, 2010), 219.

76. "The Buzz Quotables," *World* (July 22, 2006), 12.

77. Cathy Burke, "Lennon's Coat Scores," *New York Post* (December 5, 2010), http://www.nypost.com/p/news/national/lennon_coat_cores_11Zd9hhCEJO1SU14gM09aO (accessed December 19, 2010). See also Fowles, *Starstruck*, 250; Lawrence, *The Cult of Celebrity*, 16.

78. Claire Lazebnik, "Haunted by a Hollywood Starlet," *The Wall Street Journal* (June 14, 2013), M14.

79. Ferguson, *Land of Lincoln*, ix ("More books have been written about Abraham Lincoln than any other American—nearly fourteen thousand in all.").

80. Ibid., 120.

81. Ibid., 131.

82. Ibid., 137.

83. "Selling It," *Consumer Reports* (September 1998), 67.

84. http://www.societenapoleonienne.com/english/BW_endowment.htm; http://www. napoleon-series.org/ins/c_weider.html; http://en.wikipedia.org/wiki/Ben_Weider (accessed March 13, 2010).

85. William Ian Miller, *Faking It* (Cambridge: Cambridge University Press, 2003), 162-63.

Chapter 3, Efforts at Significance, Part Two

1. "Assassin's Diary," *Harper's Magazine* (January 1973), 62.

2. See http://currenteventsproductions.com/ (accessed July 29, 2009); http://www.imemories.com/ (accessed July 29, 2009).

3. Transcript, "Morning Edition" (Washington, D.C.: National Public Radio, January 27, 1994); http://en.wikipedia.org/wiki/Robert_Shields_(diarist) (accessed August 29, 2009); Douglas Martin, "Robert Shields, Wordy Diarist, Dies at 89," *New York Times* (October 29, 2007); http://www.wsulibs.wsu.edu/MASC/msaccessions.html (accessed August 29, 2009).

4. Charles Derber, *The Pursuit of Attention*, 2nd ed. (Oxford: Oxford University Press, 2000), xi, xvii, xviii.

5. Aline Mosley, "The Glory of Paris Slipping, Report Says," *The Atlanta Journal & Constitution* (July 29, 1973), 10-C.

6. Alvin Toffler, *Future Shock* (New York: Bantam, 1970), 1-3, 9-18, 343-67.

7. Robert Hughes, "Can Italy Be Saved from Itself?" *Time* (June 5, 1972), 42, 43.

8. Ian Harrison, *The Book of Firsts* (London: Octopus Publishing Group, 2003).

9. Joseph Nathan, *Famous First Facts* (New York: H. W. Wilson, 1964).

10. "Google's Mission: To Organize the World's Information and Make It Universally Accessible and Useful," http://www.google.com/intl/en/corporate/ (accessed November 14, 2009).

11. Robert Lee Hotz, "A Data Deluge Swamps Science Historians," *The Wall Street Journal* (August 28, 2009), A6.

12. Ibid.

13. Ibid.

14. Ibid.

15. Ibid.

16. "What Happened to Ted?" http://sportsillustrated.cnn.com/baseball/news/2003/08/12/williams_si/ (accessed July 4, 2009) ("Williams' son, John Henry Williams, had his father placed in cryonic suspension, a deep-freezing process done in hopes that future scientific advances will restore the dead to life." Reportedly, Williams's head and body are stored in separate containers of liquid nitrogen.).

17. Antonio Regalado, "A Cold Calculus Leads Cryonauts to Put Assets on Ice," *The Wall Street Journal* (January 21-22, 2006), 1.

18. David Segal, "This Man Is Not a Cyborg. Yet.," *The New York Times* (June 1, 2013); Lynde Langdon, "Small Science," *World*

(March 4, 2006), 32-34 ("Transhumanists believe science, including nanotechnology, will help humans transcend their mental and physical limitations, including pain and death."). See also Ramez Naam, *More Than Human: Embracing the Promise of Biological Enhancement* (New York: Broadway, 2005); Brian Alexander, *Rapture: A Raucous Tour of Cloning, Transhumanism, and the New Era of Immortality* (New York: Basic Books, 2003).

19. Fred Inglis, *A Short History of Celebrity* (Princeton, NJ: Princeton University Press, 2010), 258.

20. Tom Payne, *Fame* (New York: Picador, 2010), 239; Albert Borowitz, *Terrorism for Self-Glorification: The Herostratos Syndrome* (Kent, OH: Kent State University Press, 2005), xi-xii, xvii, 4, 6-7, 9.

21. Borowitz, *Terrorism for Self-Glorification*, 4, 9, 16, 18-19, 114-16, 120.

22. "Apartment Fire a Rescue Stunt, Prosecutors Say," http://www.free webs.com/berkshirejustice/josephstone2005.htm (accessed May 9, 2010); see also *Commonwealth v. Stone*, 70 Mass. App. Ct. 800, 803, 877 N.E.2d 620, 623 (Mass. App. Ct., 2007) (in one of his statements to the police, Stone said that he started the fire because he "felt that nobody there appreciated what [he] did or had done").

23. Some notorious examples are discussed in the text below. Others include twenty-five-year-old Kimveer Gill, who went on a shooting spree at Montreal's Dawson College and then committed suicide.

Before his rampage, Gill blogged at www.vampirefreaks.com, where he expressed some of his twisted thoughts. Although the police knew nothing of his Internet presence, he imagined that he was the subject of intense police surveillance. Gill wrote, "I know you're watching me . . . . I laugh at thee. There is nothing you can do to stop me. HA HA HA HA HA HA HA HA." http://www.slate.com/articles/news_and_politics/jurisprudence/2006/09/networking_born_killers.2.html (accessed March 22, 2013).

24. Jean M. Twenge and W. Keith Campbell, *The Narcissism Epidemic* (New York: Free Press, 2009), 195.

25. Leo Braudy, *The Frenzy of Renown* (New York: Vintage, 1997), 562.

26. "Police: Nine Killed in Shooting at Omaha Mall, Including Gunman," http://www.cnn.com/2007/US/12/05/mall.shooting/ (accessed September 15, 2009); http://en.wikipedia.org/wiki/Westroads_Mall_shooting (accessed September 15, 2009).

27. Robert A. Fein and Bryan Vossekuil, "Assassination in the United States: An Operational Study of Recent Assassins, Attackers, and Near-Lethal Approachers," *Journal of Forensic Sciences* 44 (March 1999), 321, 327-28, 331, 333; Paul E. Mullen, et al., "The Role of Psychotic Illnesses in Attacks on Public Figures," *Stalking, Threatening, and Attacking Public Figures: A Psychological and Behavioral Analysis*, ed. J. Reid Maloy, et al. (Oxford: Oxford University Press, 2008), 67.

28. "Assassin's Diary," 64.

29. Ibid., 62.

30. Ibid.

31. Ibid.

32. Ibid.

33. Ibid. (apparent reference to the Dead Sea Scrolls).

34. James Dobson, *Hide or Seek* (Grand Rapids, MI: Fleming H. Revell, 2001 [1974]), 21-23.

35. Alex Kinsbury, "The Final Verdict," *U.S. News & World Report* (June 11, 2007), 24.

36. "The Man Who Killed Kennedy," http://www.today.com/id/3541517/#.UUxrGFeyLtw (accessed March 22, 2013).

37. Jack Jones, *Let Me Take You Down: Inside the Mind of Mark David Chapman, the Man Who Killed John Lennon* (New York: Villard, 1992), 250.

38. http://www.nationmaster.com/encyclopedia/Mark-David-Chapman (accessed August 4, 2013).

39. Valerius Maximus, *Memorable Doings and Sayings* 8.14, ed. and trans. D. R. Shackleton-Bailey, Loeb Classical Library (Cambridge, MA: Harvard University Press, 2000).

40. Borowitz, *Terrorism for Self-Glorification*, 72-79.

41. http://www.nytimes.com/2007/04/18/us/18cnd-virginia.html?_r=0 (accessed April 19, 2013).

42. http://www.google.com/search?hl=en&lr=&q=%22cho+seung+hui %22&aq=f&oq=&aqi=g10 (accessed August 7, 2013).

43. Kathryn Westcott, "Cho Fits Pattern of Campus Killers," http://news.bbc.co.uk/2/hi/americas/6567143.stm (accessed August 3, 2009).

44. Gerold Frank, *The Boston Strangler* (New York: New American Library, 1966), 249, 253, 338, 339.

45. Ibid., 213.

46. http://murderpedia.org/male.R/r/rader-dennis.htm (accessed May 4, 2013); http://en.wikipedia.org/wiki/Dennis_Rader (accessed May 4, 2013).

47. Marlon Manuel, "I Confess," *The Atlanta Journal-Constitution* (August 24, 2006), A1.

48. "Police Still Seek Percy Killer," *The Atlanta Journal* (December 6, 1973), 18-F; http://en.wikipedia.org/wiki/Charles_H._Percy (accessed August 11, 2009).

49. Manuel, "I Confess," A1, A9; http://en.wikipedia.org/wiki/ John_Mark_Karr (accessed September 15, 2009).

50. Eric Berne, *Games People Play* (New York: Grove Press, 1964), 84.

51. Ibid., 111-12.

52. Ibid., 107.

53. Albert Camus, *The Plague* (New York: Modern Library, 1948), 175.

54. Berne, *Games People Play*, 75-76.

55. Ashley Montagu, "The Origin of Aggressiveness," in *Significance: The Struggle We Share*, ed. John H. Brennecke and Robert G. Amick (Beverly Hills, CA: Glencoe, 1971), 42.

56. Katharine Rosman, "Ten Years of 15 Minutes," *The Wall Street Journal* (December 21, 2009), R7.

57. Tony Cowell, *Is It Just Me or Is Everyone Famous* (London: John Blake Publishing, 2007), 56-98.

58. Ibid., 148.

59. www.celeb4aday.com (accessed December 26, 2010).

60. Twenge and Campbell, *Narcissism Epidemic*, 108-12.

61. Candice M. Kelsey, *Generation My Space* (New York: Marlowe & Company, 2007), 81.

62. Jim Green, *How to Become Famous Online: Without Spending a Dime* (2005).

63. www.iwannabefamous.com/ (accessed May 2, 2009).

64. Derber, *Pursuit of Attention*, xv.

65. Fydor Dostoyevsky, *Notes from Underground and The Double* (London: Penguin, 1972 [1864]), 15.

66. Erving Goffman, *The Presentation of Self in Everyday Life* (New York: Anchor, 1959), 252.

67. Jake Halpern, *Fame Junkies* (New York: Houghton Mifflin, 2007), xxiii.

68. Braudy, *Frenzy of Renown*, 587 n. 24.

Chapter 4, Negative Effects of the Competition for Significance

1. Oscar Wilde, "The Remarkable Rocket," in *The Happy Prince and Other Stories* (London: Penguin Group, 2009 [1888]), 46.

2. Charles Derber, *The Pursuit of Attention*, 2nd ed. (Oxford: Oxford University Press, 2000), xi-xii. See also William Ian Miller, *Faking It* (Cambridge: Cambridge University Press, 2003), 41, 164-65 (noting how self-absorption can affect social conversation and even one's experience of, for example, an art museum by leading one to posture and preen in order to be seen by other people as a sophisticated viewer).

3. Derber, *Pursuit of Attention*, xiii.

4. Ibid., xvi-xvii.

5. Jean M. Twenge and W. Keith Campbell, *The Narcissism Epidemic* (New York: Free Press, 2009), 69, 110-12, 122; Cooper Lawrence, *The Cult of Celebrity* (Guilford, Conn.; Globe Pequot Press, 2009), 51.

6. Ibid., 110.

7. Neal Gabler, *Winchell: Gossip, Power, and the Culture of Celebrity* (New York: Vintage, 1994), 86.

8. Albert Borowitz, *Terrorism for Self-Glorification: The Herostratos Syndrome* (Kent, OH: Kent State University Press, 2005), xii, xvii, 4, 6-7, 9.

9. Interview with Michael Freedland, "Al Jolson Entertained Followers, But Suffered with a Monster Ego," *The Atlanta Journal & Constitution* (December 17, 1972), 9-F.

10. Thomas Hauser, *Muhammad Ali: His Life and Times* (New York: Simon & Schuster, 1991), 399.

11. Hal Hellman, *Great Feuds in Medicine* (New York: John Wiley & Sons, 2001), 116.

12. Derber, *Pursuit of Attention*, xxiii.

13. Ibid., xxv.

14. Tony Cowell, *Is It Just Me or Is Everyone Famous* (London: John Blake Publishing, 2007), 21-25; Andrew Evans and Glenn D. Wilson, *Fame: The Psychology of Stardom* (London: Vision Paperbacks, 1999), 144-48.

Chapter 5, Human Efforts Fail to Achieve Significance

1. Tom Wolfe, *A Man in Full* (New York: Farrar Straus Giroux, 1998), 659.

2. For a thorough review of the history of fame and its mechanisms, see Leo Braudy, *The Frenzy of Renown* (New York: Vintage, 1997). See also Jake Halpern, *Fame Junkies* (New York: Houghton Mifflin, 2007), xxi; Andrew Evans and Glenn D. Wilson, *Fame: The Psychology of Stardom* (London: Vision Paperbacks, 1999), 15-16.

3. Braudy, *Frenzy of Renown*, 5.

4. Evans and Wilson, *Fame*, 18, 23, noting that in 1998 the vast majority of obituaries reported in London newspapers were for entertainers. See also Jib Fowles, *Starstruck* (Washington, D.C.: Smithsonian Institution, 1992), 11-12, 120-121, 165.

5. See Alan Schwarz, "'The Greatest': What a Concept," *The New York Times* (June 13, 2009).

6. Thomas Ayres, *That's Not in My American History Book: a compilation of little-known events and forgotten heroes*, (Lanham, Maryland: Taylor Trade Publishing, 2000), 8-9; http://www.cbs news.com/8301-504803_162-57599046-10391709/update-wright-is-wrong/ (accessed August 19, 2013).

7. http://www.census.gov/ipc/www/popclockworld.html (accessed August 15, 2009).

8. Carl Haub, "How Many People Have Ever Lived on Earth?" *Population Today* 30, no. 8 (Population Reference Bureau; November/December 2002), 3–4, http://www.prb.org/Articles /2002/HowManyPeopleHaveEverLivedonEarth.aspx (accessed March 22, 2013). See also http://www.census.gov/ipc/ www/worldhis.html (accessed August 15, 2009); Cecil Adams, *More of the Straight Dope* (New York: Ballantine, 1988), 85-86 ("The more reputable demographers, equipped with the latest tools of science, say there have been between 69 billion and 110 billion humans.").

9. John H. M. Hallock, *The American Byron* (Madison: University of Wisconsin Press, 2000), 5-6.

10. Marvin Olasky, "Fleeting Fame," *World* (July 28, 2007), 29.

11. Dante Alighieri, *The Divine Comedy of Dante Alighieri: Hell, Purgatory, Paradise*, trans. Henry F. Cary (New York: P. F. Collier & Son, 1909 [1321]), vol. 20:189.

12. Stephen Stigler, "Stigler's Law of Eponymy," in *Science and Social Structure: A Festschrift for Robert K. Merton*, ed. T. F. Gieryn (New York: New York Academy of Sciences, 1980), 147-57. See also http://en.wikipedia.org/wiki/Stigler's_law_of_ eponymy (accessed August 16, 2009); http://en.wikipedia.org/wiki /List_of_examples_of_Stigler%27s_law (accessed August 16, 2009); H. C. Kennedy, *American Mathematics Monthly* 79 (1972), 66-67 ("mathematical formulas and theorems are usually not named after their original discoverers").

13. John Bemelmans Marciano, *Anonyponymous: The Forgotten People Behind Everyday Words* (New York: Bloomsbury, 2009), 136. The author coins the term "anonyponymous" to refer to people who are no longer remembered as the source of an eponymous word.

14. Ibid., 3.

15. http://en.wikipedia.org/wiki/Lemuel_P._Grant (accessed September 22, 2009).

16. Rick Hampson, "Roads, Bridges, You Name It . . .," *USA Today* (March 3, 2006), 3A, http://www.usatoday.com/news/nation/2006-03-02-bridges-roads-names_x.htm (accessed September 25, 2009).

17. Ibid.

18. Ibid.

19. Boethius, *The Consolation of Philosophy*, trans. H. R. James (London: Elliot Stock, 1897 [ca. 526]), 79-80.

20. Howard Albert Johnson, *Kierkegaard: An Introduction* (n.p.: Forward Movement Publications, n.d.).

21. Percy Bysshe Shelley, "Ozymandias," in *The Top 500 Poems*, ed. William Harmon (New York: Columbia University Press, 1992), 495.

22. Sir Thomas Browne, *Selected Writings*, ed. Claire Preston (New York: Routledge, 2003 [1658]), 105, 107.

23. Robert Hughes, "Can Italy Be Saved from Itself?" *Time* (June 5, 1972), 42, 43.

24. Albert Camus, *The Myth of Sisyphus* (New York: Random House, 1955), 66.

25. Albert Camus, *The Plague* (New York: Modern Library, 1948), 5.

26. Thomas Gray, "Elegy Written in a Country Churchyard," in *The Top 500 Poems*, ed. William Harmon (New York: Columbia University Press, 1992), 327-29.

Chapter 6, The Persistent Yearning for Significance

1. *Humanist Manifestos I and II* (Buffalo, NY: Prometheus, 1973), 14-15.

2. Bertrand Russell, *Why I Am Not a Christian and Other Essays on Religion and Related Subjects*, ed. Paul Edwards (New York: Simon & Schuster, 1957), 107.

3. Peter Singer, *Animal Liberation*, rev. ed. (New York: Avon Books, 1975), 1, 19.

4. Jean-Paul Sartre, *Being and Nothingness* (New York: Kensington, 1956), 523.

5. "Declaration of the United Nations Conference on the Human Environment," http://www.unep.org/Documents.Multilingual/Default.asp?documentid=97&articleid=1503 (accessed March 23, 2013).

6. *Humanist Manifestos I and II*, 18.

7. C. S. Lewis, *Mere Christianity* (New York: Macmillan, 1952), 28.

8. John Stuart Mill, *Three Essays on Religion* (Amherst, NY: Prometheus, 1998), 122.

9. [Judith Sargent Murray], "The Reaper," no. 5 in the *Federal Orrery* (Boston: November 20, 1794).

10. Miguel de Unamuno, *Tragic Sense of Life*, trans. J. E. Crawford Flitch (New York: Dover Publications, 2011 [1912]), 25.

11 Ibid., 30.

12. Paul Bowles, *The Sheltering Sky* (New York: Harper Collins, 1949), 238.

13. Roy Arundhati, *The God of Small Things* (New York: Random House, 1997), 1.

14. http://www.cdc.gov/nchs/fastats/lifexpec.htm (accessed November 15, 2009).

15. See, e.g., *Louis, I.M. & S. Ry. v. Craft*, 237 U.S. 648, 35 Sup. Ct. 704 (1915).

16. See *Jones v. Billings*, 289 A.2d 39, 40 (Maine Supreme Ct., 1972) (recognizing a claim for "alleged wrongful death and conscious suffering" of "child, aged three years, [who] climbed or fell into a cesspool on the premises of the defendant," which was allegedly "negligently left open and unprotected by the defendant").

17. Francis A. Schaeffer, *The God Who Is There* (Downers Grove, IL: InterVarsity Press, 1968), 89.

Chapter 7, Made in the Image of God

1. Philosopher Alvin Plantinga argues that the conjunction of naturalism (i.e., there are no supernatural beings) and "contemporary evolutionary theory" are self-defeating for "any belief produced by our cognitive faculties." See Alvin Plantinga, *Warrant and Proper Function* (New York: Oxford University Press, 1993), 229-30; Alvin Plantinga, "Introduction," in

Naturalism Defeated, ed. James Beilby (Ithaca, NY: Cornell University Press, 2002), 1-12, 204-75.

2. Bertrand Russell, *Why I am Not a Christian and Other Essays on Religion and Related Subjects*, ed. Paul Edwards (New York: Simon & Schuster, 1957), 107.

3. Friedrich Nietzsche, *Beyond Good and Evil* (New York: Random House, 1966), 85.

4. Arthur C. Danto, *Nietzsche as Philosopher* (New York: Macmillan, 1965), 223.

5. Friedrich Wilhelm Nietzsche, *The Will to Power (Volumes I and II)*, 2010 [1901]), 145; Celine Rita Jette, *The Philosophy of Nietzsche in the Light of Thomistic Principles* (New York: Pageant Press, 1967), 20.

6. Nietzsche, *The Will to Power*, 330.

7. Adam Gottlieb, *The Pleasures of Cocaine* (Berkeley, CA: Ronin, 1976), 18.

8. Ibid., 18-19.

9. Aleister Crowley, *The Book of the Law: Liber Al Vel Legis* (York Beach, ME: Red Wheel/Weiser, 2004 [1904]), 13.

10. "Aleister Crowley—The Muse of Rock and Roll," http://www.zimbio.com/Aleister+Crowley/articles/6/Aleister+Cro wley+Muse+Rock+Roll (accessed December 19, 2010).

11. Richard Kaczynski, *Perdurabo: The Life of Aleister Crowley* (Berkeley, CA: North Atlantic Books, 2002), 63, 65, 179, 197,

203, 211, 216, 273, 458; Lawrence Sutin, *Do What Thou Wilt: A Life of Aleister Crowley* (New York: St. Martin's Griffin, 2002), 45-46, 63-64, 128-29, 158-59, 183-86, 198, 217, 228, 292; Aleister Crowley, *The Diary of a Drug Fiend* (York Beach, ME: Samuel Weiser, 1970 [1922]).

12. John Powers, *A Concise Introduction to Tibetan Buddhism* (Ithaca, NY: Snow Lion Publications, 2008), 49, 132-33. See also Steve Hagen, *Buddhism Is Not What You Think: Finding Freedom Beyond Beliefs* (New York: Harper Collins, 2003), 78-79, 112-13, 135, 204, 220-21.

13. Jesse De Boer, "First Steps in Mysticism," in *Faith and Philosophy*, ed. Alvin Plantinga (Grand Rapids, MI: Eerdmans, 1964), 66-93; Jingjing Z. Edmondson, "Life and Immortality: A Comparison of Scientific, Christian, and Hindu Concepts," *Life Science Journal* (2005), 2, 4-5.

14. Powers, *Concise Introduction to Tibetan Buddhism*, 36, 145; Hillary Rodrigues, *Introducing Hinduism* (New York: Routledge, 2006), 52-53 ("The Buddhist notion of *nirvāna* is akin to *moksa*, since both refer to the goal of emancipation or freedom from *karma* and *samsāra*, and insight into the true nature of reality and the Self.").

15. Karl Marx, *A Contribution to the Critique of Political Economy*, trans. N. I. Stone (Chicago: Kerr, 1904), 268 ("Man is in the most literal sense of the word . . . not only a social animal, but an animal

which can develop into an individual only in society"); Karl Marx, *Selected Works* (London: Lawrence and Wishart, 1948), vol. 1:472-73 [MEGA I/5, 535]; Georg Lukás, *Geschichte und Klassenbewusstsein* (Germany: Sammlung Luchterhand, 1968), quoted in Adam Schaff, *Marxism and the Human Individual* (New York: McGraw-Hill, 1970), 61-62.

16. Soon Ok Lee, *Eyes of the Tailless Animals* (Bartlesville, OK: Living Sacrifice Book, 1999), 52.

17. Katie McCabe, "Who Will Live, Who Will Die?" *Washingtonian* (August 1986), 21, quoted in Wesley J. Smith, *A Rat Is a Pig Is a Dog Is a Boy* (New York: Encounter Books, 2010), 3.

18. Miguel de Unamuno, *Tragic Sense of Life*, trans. J. E. Crawford Flitch (New York: Dover Publications, 2011 [1912]), 8.

Chapter 8, Known by the Omnipresent, Eternal, and Omniscient God

1. In another passage, Paul says that he is "well known to God" (2 Corinthians 5:11 NKJV).

2. Bruce K. Waltke, *Finding the Will of God* (Grand Rapids, MI: Eerdmans, 2002), 130-31.

3. Another example is Daniel's ability, through divine revelation, to tell King Nebuchadnezzar both what the king dreamed and what it meant (Daniel 2). There are also many examples of Jesus knowing

the thoughts of persons. For instance, Jesus was aware of the secret reasoning of the scribes who were skeptical of his statement that the sins of a paralytic were forgiven (Mark 2:5-11).

4. See also Matthew 6:2-8, 16-18.

5. See also Psalm 90:8; Proverbs 5:21.

6. See also Matthew 6:4, 6.

7. Charles Hodge, *Systematic Theology*, 3 vols. (reprint ed.; Grand Rapids, MI: Eerdmans, 1975), 1:397.

8. Alexis de Tocqueville, *Democracy in America*, trans. Henry Reeve (New York: Random House, 2002 [1835]), 522.

9. The descendants of Ishmael and his half-brother Isaac have been locked in constant enmity ever since.

10. See also Galatians 3:28; 1 Corinthians 12:13.

11. Genesis 21:2; 25:21; 30:22-24; Judges 13:2-3; 1 Samuel 1:5, 20; Luke 1:5, 7, 11-14.

Chapter 9, God Interacts with Individual People

1. See also Psalms 100:5; 107:1; 118:1; 135:3; 136:1.

2. See also Isaiah 9:17.

3. See also Nehemiah 9:17; Psalm 130:3-4.

4. See also 1 Kings 3:14; 11:4, 6.

5. Kenneth N. Taylor, *Is Christianity Credible?* (Downers Grove, IL: InterVarsity Press, 1970), 25.

6. See also Romans 10:9-10.

7. See also Revelation 4:10-11.

8. See also Matthew 19:27-30.

9. See also Ecclesiastes 12:13-14.

10. See also Job 9:19.

11. See also 1 Kings 11:14, 23, 25; 2 Kings 24:1-3; 2 Chronicles 12:1-5; 13:13-17; Isaiah 10:5-7.

12. See Judges 3:7-8, 12-14; 4:1-2; 6:1-6; 10:6-8; 13:1; 2 Kings 13:2-3; 17:6-8, 18; 24:20; 25:8-9, 13-14; 1 Chronicles 5:25-26; 6:15; 2 Chronicles 24:23-24; 28:1, 5; 33:10-11; 36:17, 20-21.

13. See Numbers 11:34-34; 25:1-9; 2 Samuel 24:15, 17; 2 Kings 15:1-5; 2 Chronicles 21:15, 18-19; 26:16-21.

14. See 2 Samuel 21:1; 1 Kings 17:1; Isaiah 3:1.

15. See Genesis 38:7; Leviticus 10:1-2; Numbers 11:1-3, 18-20; 21:4-9; 1 Samuel 25:38; 2 Samuel 6:6-7; 1 Kings 11:13-31; 20:35-36; 2 Kings 1:9-12; 2 Chronicles 13:20; Psalm 73:18-20; Isaiah 3:1-5.

16. See also Deuteronomy 11:16-17; 29:22-28; 1 Kings 17:1; 2 Kings 3:4-5, 18-19, 24-25; Isaiah 10:33-34.

17. See also 1 Peter 2:24; Isaiah 53:5-6, 10-12.

18. See also 1 Chronicles 16:31-33; Romans 8:19-22.

Chapter 10, People Live Forever After Death

1. Albert Camus, *The Plague* (New York: Modern Library, 1948), 70.

2. See also Ecclesiastes 12:7; Deuteronomy 32:48-50; Judges 2:10; 2 Samuel 12:23; Job 19:26.

3. C. S. Lewis, *The Weight of Glory and Other Addresses* (New York: Harper Collins, 1949), 170-71.

4. Charles Hartshorne, *The Logic of Perfection* (LaSalle, IL: Open Court, 1962), 249, 250.

5. Ibid., 262.

6. Ibid., 253.

7. *Humanist Manifestos I and II* (Buffalo, NY: Prometheus, 1973), 17.

Chapter 11, Individual Human Significance Is Complete

1. C. S. Lewis, *The Weight of Glory and Other Addresses* (New York: Harper Collins, 1949), 45-46.

2. Ira Flatow, *They All Laughed* (New York: Harper Collins, 1993), 71-84.

3. Michael Farquhar, *A Treasury of Foolishly Forgotten Americans* (New York: Penguin, 2008), 25-29.

4. Robert S. McGee, *The Search for Significance* (Houston: Rapha Publishing, 1990), 158.

5. See Matthew 26:63; 27:12-14; John 19:8-9.

Chapter 12, Length of Life Does Not Affect the Significance of a Person

1. Ben Johnson, in *Sound and Sense: An Introduction to Poetry*, ed. Laurence Perrine (New York: Harcourt, Brace & World, 1969 [1640]), 29.

2. William Blake, *Selected Poetry and Prose of William Blake*, ed. Northrop Frye (New York: Modern Library, 1953 [ca. 1791-92]), 63.

Chapter 13, Popularity Is of No Account

1. George Eliot, *Middlemarch* (Oxford: Oxford University Press, 1996), 785.

2. http://www.wanpela.com/holdouts/list.html (accessed December 13, 2009); http://en. wikipedia.org/wiki/Hiroo_Onoda (accessed December 13, 2009).

3. Andrew Ferguson, *Land of Lincoln* (New York: Grove Press, 2007), ix (fourteen thousand books have been written about Lincoln).

4. Tyler Cowen, *What Price Fame?* (Cambridge, MA: Harvard University Press, 2000), 51-52, (noting the near "deification" of Washington after his death, with images of him found in many homes—and numerous cities, counties, geographical features, colleges, and so on, named for him).

5. http://en.wikipedia.org/wiki/Elmer_mccurdy (accessed August 18, 2009).

6. Patricia Guthrie, " 'John Doe No. 1': After Three Years, Identity Still a Mystery," *The Atlanta Journal & Constitution* (July 31, 2005), http://www2.accessnorthga.com/detail.php?n=129152 (accessed September 3, 2009).

7. Chuck Swindoll refers to these persons as the "willing unknowns" of Scripture. As an example, he cites the description in Nehemiah 11:12 of 822 unknown persons "who performed the work of the temple." Charles R. Swindoll, *Hand Me Another Brick* (Nashville: W Publishing Group, 1998), 157-68.

8. See Vern Poythress, "A 'Day of Small Things,' " *World* (March 8-15, 2008), 64 (urging Christians to be content in being faithful in what may appear to be small things).

9. See also Philippians 3:17; 4:9; 1 Thessalonians 1:6; 2 Thessalonians 3:7-9.

10. See also Romans 14:8; 1 Corinthians 10:31.

Chapter 14, Treat People Equally

1. See also Proverbs 24:23.

2. See Acts 10:34; Romans 2:11; Galatians 2:6; Ephesians 6:9; James 2:1, 9.

3. C. S. Lewis, *The Great Divorce* (New York: Macmillan, 1946), 83.

4. See also 1 Samuel 2:10.

5. See also Proverbs 20:28.

6. See also Ezra 10:4; Isaiah 1:23; 9:13-16; 10:1-4; Matthew 5:19; 7:1-5.

7. See Exodus 18:25-26; Numbers 11:16-17; Deuteronomy 1:15; 16:18; 18:14-16; 20:9; 1 Samuel 8:12; 2 Samuel 18:1-2; 1 Kings 5:16; 2 Kings 11:18; 1 Chronicles 6:31-32; 9:22-24, 31; 15:28; 16:4-6; 27:1, 25-31; 2 Chronicles 31:11-14; Ezra 3:8; Nehemiah 10:38; 12:8; Acts 6:1-6.

8. See also Ecclesiastes 8:2-5; Matthew 17:24-27; 22:15-21; Romans 13:1-7; Titus 3:1; 1 Peter 2:13-15.

9. See also Psalm 149:2.

Chapter 15, Records Are Unessential

1. C. S. Lewis, *Surprised by Joy* (New York: Harcourt Brace Jovanovich, 1955), 226.

2. See also Deuteronomy 6:1-9.

3. See also Psalm 119:16, 83.

4. See also Deuteronomy 27:1-4, 8; Joshua 8:30-32.

5. See also Deuteronomy 32:6-7; 1 Chronicles 16:12.

6. See also Deuteronomy 7:17-18; Judges 5:11.

7. See also Exodus 17:14-16; Joshua 24:24-27; Judges 6:23-24; 1 Samuel 7:12.

Chapter 16, Free to Be Humble, Forgive, and Love Others

1. See also Matthew 11:29.

2. Walter C. Langer, *The Mind of Adolf Hitler* (New York: Basic Books, 1972), 30.

3. See also Romans 12:10.

4. See also Romans 14:13-15, 20-21.

5. See also Mark 1:35-38.

6. Ronald Eisenberg, *The JPS Guide to Jewish Traditions* (Philadelphia: Jewish Publication Society, 2004), 537; http://www.jewfaq.org/tzedakah.htm (accessed October 6, 2009), discussing the levels of tzedakah.

7. See also Matthew 5:43-47.

8. Richard Wurmbrand, *Tortured for Christ* (Glendale, CA: Diane Books, 1969), 54.

9. Jean M. Twenge and W. Keith Campbell, *The Narcissism Epidemic* (New York: Free Press, 2009), 57-69.

10. See also 1 Samuel 30:10, 21-25.

11. See also Matthew 5:42; Luke 6:30.

12. See also Mark 11:25.

13. Benjamin Jowett, trans., *The Dialogues of Plato* (Chicago: Encyclopedia Britannica, 1952), 293.

Chapter 17, Free to Enjoy the Purpose of Life

1. G. I. Williamson, *The Westminster Shorter Catechism: For Study Classes* (Phillipsburg, NJ: P&R Publishing, 1970 [1643-1652]), 1.

2. See also 1 Timothy 6:16-19; 2 Peter 1:3.

3. See also Matthew 10:39.

4. See also Romans 14:6-8; Colossians 3:17.

5. See also Exodus 34:28; Matthew 6:25; Mark 2:15-17; John 4:34; Romans 14:6-8.

6. See also Acts 21:13.

7. See also Philippians 2:17; 2 Timothy 4:6.

8. Charles R. Swindoll, *Hand Me Another Brick* (Nashville: W Publishing Group, 1998), 157-68.

9. Oswald Chambers, *My Utmost for His Highest* (New York: Dodd, Mead, 1935), 295 (October 21).

10. See also Hebrews 11:1.

11. See also Hebrews 11:13, 39.

12. Acts 17:2-3; 18:28.

13. C. S. Lewis, *The Weight of Glory and Other Addresses* (New York: Harper Collins, 1949), 46.

Index

A

B

C

court, 126, 155, 158
Cowell, Tony, 230, 232
Cowen, Tyler, 29
craftsmen, 162
credit, 15, 17, 20, 25, 34-35, 37, 49, 62, 152, 196, 198
crime, criminal, iii, 17, 24, 37, 43-44, 48-49, 57, 105, 199
Crowley, Aleister, 94
crown, 14, 32, 117, 125
crucified, crucifixion, 182, 205, 207
Crutchlow, Kenneth, 19
cryonic, cryonauts, 42
culture, iii, 27, 38, 40-41, 54, 56, 68, 137, 140
curator, 41
curse, cursed, 96, 128-129, 196

D

Dali, Salvador, 7
Dalits, 160
Daniel, Old Testament character, 241
Danto, Arthur C., 238
Darrow, Clarence, 28
Davey, 17
David, King, 22, 29, 59, 99, 102-105, 107, 112, 118, 121, 123, 126-127, 130, 163, 165, 168, 173, 183, 185-186, 195-196, 204
daVinci, Leonardo, 43
Davis, John M., 22
Dawes, William, 149
De Salvo, Albert, 49
de Tocqueville, Alexis, 241
de Unamuno, Miguel, 11, 13, 83-84, 96
Dean's List, 16
Dean, Dizzy, 24
death, iv, xii, 11, 16, 19, 21, 44, 70, 81, 84, 86, 121, 124, 129, 135-143, 155, 157, 184, 206
defer, deferring, 110, 191

J

K

L

M

N

O

Q,R

Stephen (New Testament character), 199
steps, 74, 103, 204, 239
Stewart, Rod, 27
Stigler, Stephen, 71
Stolen Valor Act, 17
storage, 38, 41, 162
stores, 95
Stossel, John, 220
Streisand, Barbara, 30
struggle, vii, 7, 11, 45, 58, 104, 136, 155
Stuarts, 15
submit, 118, 193
succeed, success, 19, 47-48, 58, 63, 165
succession, 15, 66
suicide, 15, 45, 61, 227
superficial, superficially, 53, 68, 76
superiority, 170
superlatives, 13
supernatural, 113, 194, 196, 208
surpass, 26
surrender, 197-198, 201
survival, survive, survivor, 7, 12, 51, 69, 75, 83, 85-86, 139, 142
swaggering, 54
swift, swiftly, 5, 66
Swindoll, Charles, 208
synagogue, 50, 113, 164
syndrome, 32

T

tabernacle, 162, 179
tabloid, 53, 58
Talmud, 195
Taper, Louise, 31
target, targeted, vii, 11, 27, 46, 59
Tasman, A.J., 71; see also Tasmania

U

X,Y,Z

CPSIA information can be obtained at www.ICGtesting.com
Printed in the USA
LVOW08s2342050214

372561LV00004B/150/P